God's People in Transition

GOD'S PEOPLE IN TRANSITION

Dan Ivins

BROADMAN PRESS
Nashville, Tennessee

4269-32
ISBN: 0-8054-6932-x

Dewey Decimal Classification: 220.92
Subject heading: BIBLE - BIOGRAPHY
Library of Congress Catalog Card Number: 80-65971

Printed in the United States of America

To Libby—my closest companion along the way.
Without her support I probably would have accomplished
very little.

Acknowledgments

Appreciation is extended to the following people for their assistance in the publication of this book. To Larry McSwain, professor and friend, who took the time to plow through the manuscript offering helpful suggestions toward making it better. To Gloria Newton, a wonderful secretary, whose tireless work always encourages me. To Dottie McGee, for help in getting difficult-to-find books from the Library of Congress. To Mary Kathryn Black, who more than any other person has provided me the opportunity and support to write. And to my good friend, Barry Click, whose wise counsel was always valuable.

These people are more than teachers, friends, and fellow strugglers. They have provided truth for my doubts, strength for my weaknesses, but more than anything else . . . they believed in me.

Preface

America has always been a nation on the move. The westward conquest of succeeding waves of new residents tapping the resources of a bountiful land brought affluence, power, and ingenuity into the American psyche. The mobility of the past two generations has been different, however. No longer does the unidirectional pilgrimage to the West bring to one unpopulated land, a frontier for exploitation, or a place for planting roots in virgin soil. Even Alaska has been purchased by the corporate geologists.

Consequently, the mobility which fulfills dreams today is "stop-over" mobility. In the past a pioneer moved to a new place to start traditions, sink roots, provide a heritage for the family. Today's mobicentric family achieves by refusing heritage, rejecting roots, and adjusting to ever-changing communities, corporations, and covenants of family, religion, and values.

The church is often one of those forgotten covenants of a stable past which is left behind in the process of movement. Dan Ivins has shown in this book the folly of such a valueless existence. Here is the proclamation of the word that faith belongs in every context, including the context of motion. For faith is a pilgrimage which strengthens one for the journey of life, whatever its demands.

The church has often identified only with that half of the population which chooses to stay put. Here is a contemporary word for those who have discovered the horizon of new frontiers in changing places, changing jobs, and changing values—

the apartment resident, the corporate climber, the military transferee, the student, the questing single. Ivins is a pastor who knows the heartbeat of change, for he has experienced it himself. But more importantly, he knows the necessity of foundations, values, an internal center, and an eternal presence that every pilgrim requires for meaningful life. He lives as a pastor to "mobiphiles" to bring the permanent word of faith to people on the move.

I commend this book to you. It is as fresh as the morning news for it addresses us in the language of today. Yet it is as eternal as the biblical revelation itself for it is rooted in the lives of those who have found a word from the Lord in the midst of their mobility. Brave journey as you walk in faith.

LARRY MCSWAIN
The Southern Baptist Theological Seminary
January, 1980

Contents

Introduction

One of the big news stories of the summer of 1979 was created by the concern about NASA's infamous Skylab, which finally disintegrated and plunged into the Indian Ocean and the southern part of Australia.[1] Is this failure of modern technology not a symbol of human existence as we know it today? We are all travelers in orbit; constantly on the move. Consequently, we live in the midst of situations that threaten to annihilate us. We wonder if our life will fall apart from the forces we encounter.

Such are the problems faced by a nation on the move. Hastened by postwar mobility, we spend much of our lives searching . . . for education, employment, housing, and opportunity. Our swelling cities have brought on social change at a rapid rate.

The resulting rootlessness can be detrimental to the quality of life as we know it. It has led to the separation of families by thousands of miles, depriving children of their grandparents and thus, a living link with the past. No longer do our children turn to their elders for guidance. Instead they turn on the television, today's indispensable tool, funneling ideas that shape upcoming generations. Here are some of the ways that "skylab earth" is disintegrating. Life-styles have become freewheeling. Participation in church has declined. Traditional values are unraveling. Family structures are becoming fragile. Before the war, there was one divorce for every 114 married couples. Today's transient society has more than doubled to one divorce for every forty-five marriages. Even young females are having their

13

babies on the move. Many don't even take the time to get married. More than a half-million babies were born to illegitimate parents in 1977, compared to 90,000 in 1940. Juvenile delinquency has increased proportionately.

One questions how our nation is moving. But moving we are. About forty million Americans change their home address each year. The average American moves about fourteen times in a lifetime. This high mobility rate can be attributed to a rise in technology, but its results are symbolized by the falling of Skylab—a society with torn-up roots, facing the prospect of falling apart.

When I was twelve years old my parents built a modern ranch-style house across town and I was uprooted from the quaint little neighborhood of my childhood days where I had enmassed quite a history. There I endured several dogs and cats, a goat which led me into the canal where I ate the ice in the winter, two sweethearts, and a terrible explosion. My grandfather's automobile was maliciously wired with nitroglycerin in a cowardly act of murder. I was only twelve, but the roots were deep.

The move wasn't so bad because I still had my friends nearby. In fact, I moved closer to some of them and the high school I attended was within walking distance. But that was my first experience with transience. It was in 1954.

Since then I have moved eight times in twenty-four years. My wife Libby and I left Tennessee to make our home in South Carolina where our two daughters were born. After six years there I entered the ministry which precipitated another move back to college in Tennessee. The next step was to seminary in Kentucky. We stayed there for three months. Then I became the minister of a country church in southern Indiana. Currently our roots are planted deep in metropolitan Maryland soil.

Living in suburban Maryland has brought on my most serious struggle with transience. What we experience here is far different from the move across town as a twelve-year-old. Living here has caused ambiguous feelings to rise within me. By nature I look forward to change and have had little trouble putting down roots wherever I have lived. But I have never gotten used to the shock of mobility that is common in the D.C. area. Government workers move in and out of this place at an incredible rate. Some of them don't even stay long enough to get their names in the local telephone book before they're gone again! Needless to say, this affects the ministry of the church. The turnover rate in membership makes it difficult to provide continuity. My family has only been here six years and already we are considered "old-timers." However, our experience with transition is mild compared to some of the people I've met. At least we have a home base and don't have to keep moving. But Vance Packard suspects that the phrase "hometown" will soon fade from our vocabulary. In his book *A Nation of Strangers,* he writes:

The impact of transience and other causes of social fragmentation affects the way people behave. It seems to me that, though we are finding that we can adjust to a rootless style of life, we must not become a society that has learned to be rootless. Rootlessness encourages shallowness in personal relationships and indifference to community problems. It contributes to a personal sense of powerlessness and insignificance and encourages hedonism as a life style.[2]

Since transition seems to be a common experience, I felt the need to write this book. It was written from the viewpoint of a Christian minister who deals with the problems of transience almost daily. I believe church fellowship and Christian teaching offer some viable alternatives to the loneliness, fragmentation, depersonalization, and hedonism caused by rootlessness.

Currently Village Baptist Church where I am minister is in transition. The several homes which have housed our ministry for eleven years have been sold as we undergo the process of moving to a new building. Seeing all the fears and apprehensions kicked up by this project has caused me to focus on transition. When I turned to the biblical word, I was surprised upon discovering so many personalities who struggled with the same thing in their own day. We have much to learn from these people of God. Each personality has a main point to teach us about his or her struggle with transience. In the conclusion to the book the focus is upon the unchangeable nature of God in the midst of a world full of turbulence. We have a firm foundation upon which we can depend in trying times . . . a God who is the same today, yesterday, and forever.

Throughout each chapter I refer to several synonyms for transition. I call it the meantime, a little while, transience, waiting, the interim, detours, leftovers, transplanted, and uprooted. These terms refer to the same experience.

Paul Tournier captured the idea as well as anyone with his model of the trapeze artist.[3] High above the crowd in a huge tent swings a trapeze artist. Like Skylab, he is constantly in motion—moving back and forth on his swing. His task is to build up the momentum necessary to transfer from one trapeze to the next. The anxiety occurs (which Tournier calls "the middle way"), the moment he lets go of one trapeze handle and hangs there suspended in midair, letting go of the security that held him safely and reaching out for the next trapeze bar, which hopefully will swing within his grasp. It is that letting go and reaching out with nothing underneath which describes the anxiety of transition. The trapeze artist stands a chance of falling to the floor and going to pieces like Skylab.

If we can't learn to handle such critical periods of life, we may find ourselves only half alive. To face this great task demands a great faith. Thus, the church can play a crucial role for our day as never before. Walter Rauschenbusch said it well around the turn of the century when he wrote:

A great task demands a great faith. To live a great life a man needs a great cause to which he can surrender, something divinely large and engrossing for which he can live and, if need be, die. A great religious faith will lift him out of his narrow grooves and make him the inspired instrument of the universal will of God. Our entire generation needs a faith, for it is confronting the mightiest task ever undertaken consciously by any generation. Our civilization is passing through a great historic transition. We are at the parting of the ways. The final outcome may be the decay and extinction of Western civilization, or it may be a new epoch in the evolution of the race . . . . Our moral efficiency depends upon our religious faith.[4]

Jesus put it this way, "I was a stranger and you welcomed me" (Matt. 25:35). According to the census bureau that casts an amazing number of folks in the role of stranger. It makes the church's responsibility in welcoming these strangers enormous. Life goes on in spite of transition. All things will happen to people—life and death, joy and sorrow, love and loss, happiness and tragedy. Since we all must come to the end of transition, some circumstances will be final. But for the time in between what all things do to us depends to a large extent on what is in us. It is my belief that religious faith has something to offer our "nation of strangers," who try to cope with transition.

One of the popular songs a few years ago was a product of such a time, entitled "Ramblin' Man." The writer says he was:

Born in the back seat of a Greyhound bus,
    rollin' down Highway 41.
Lord I was born a ramblin' man.
Trying to make a living and doing the best I can.
But when it's time for leaving,
I hope you'll understand,
    that Lord I was born a ramblin' man.[5]

That is the purpose of this book—to try to help us understand ramblin' people.

---

[1]"Skylab's Fiery Finish," by Tom Riggert, *National Geographic Magazine,* Vol 156, No. 4, October 1979, pp. 581-584.

[2]Reprinted with permission from the book *A Nation of Strangers* (p. 270) by Vance Packard, copyright 1972 by Vance Packard. Published by David McKay Co., Inc.

[3]Paul Tournier, *A Place for You* (New York: Harper & Row Publishers, Inc., 1968), p. 162.

[4]Walter Rauschenbusch, *Christianizing the Social Order* (New York: copyright 1912 by Macmillan Publishing Company, Inc., renewed 1940 by Pauline Rauschenbusch), p. 40. Reprinted with the permission of the publisher.

[5]Used by permission of Capicorn Records, 535 Cotton Ave., Macon, Georgia 31201.

1
Cain: Passing Through the Doors

"I am the door; if any one enters by me, he will be saved, and will go in and out and find pasture" (John 10:9).

The door is a frequent model in the Bible because it is such a clear symbol. Genesis 4:7 (KJV) reminds us that "sin lieth at the door." In Revelation there is an open door which no one can shut. Jesus also is pictured standing outside a door and knocking. One of the graphic instances involving a door in Christian history was that fateful day when Martin Luther tacked his Ninety-five Theses on the door of Wittenberg Church, which set off the Protestant Reformation.

The door still retains this clarity of symbolism. In the last decade we saw Governor George Wallace defiantly blocking the door at the University of Alabama (later to open the doors). Pope John symbolically opened the doors of the Roman Catholic Church at Vatican II.

Life is a series of doors opening and closing. Sometimes we can open the doors and go back. Other times the closed door is irrevocable. Such was the situation at the close of Genesis 3. "Therefore the Lord God sent him forth from the garden of Eden, to till the ground from which he was taken. He drove out the man; and at the east of the garden of Eden he placed the cherubim, and a flaming sword which turned every way, to guard the way to the tree of life" (vv. 23-24).

Adam and Eve had to turn away from all they knew and were familiar with to pursue an unknown future. The east gate was sealed. This time there was no going back. And there stood

Adam—outside the Garden. Was he not a symbol of every person? Curious about sin, we sample the fruit and from that time on face the consequences of our choice. We, too, go beyond the point of no return. We are struggling with transition. The door is shut. We understand very well the parable Jesus told of the foolish virgins who missed the banquet. It is final. There is no going back.

Now, once we are outside of "Eden" and innocence is lost, our circumstance is somewhat determined. It is then that our attitude becomes crucial, for that is about the only thing that is not determined. How will we respond to that which we cannot change? How will we react to being uprooted from the familiar and thrust into the unfamiliar? Our response determines whether the door becomes a barrier to block us from happiness or a passageway to enter on the pilgrimage toward fulfillment.

Adam's first son, Cain, didn't do so well. In fact, he let the meantime get the best of him because of a poor attitude. Through a mishandling of his negative emotions, Cain provides us with an interesting study of both external and internal conflict and its consequences. He began at the east of Eden and continued into the land of Nod, the land of wandering.

Genesis 4 provides us with the dynamics of interpersonal relationships: conflict and rivalry, competition and struggle, fear and pressure . . . daily companions of those in the midst of transition. Feelings come to the surface. There is anger, jealousy, suspicion, hatred, pain, stubbornness, and the refusal to be consoled. The result of mishandling these negative emotions is the same as it was in Cain's day—alienation. Breakdown and division occur between people who ought to be close to one another.

The Cause of Conflict

First let's consider the cause of Cain's conflict. The story begins with the birth of two sons to Adam and Eve. Both were born outside of Eden. Cain, the eldest, whose name means "spear" or "metal worker," was a farmer. Abel, "breath-puff," was a shepherd and tended the flocks. The two different ways of life chosen by the sons indicates a secondary vocational conflict, but the real conflict was religious. Abel knew how to worship. Cain didn't. When they both brought offerings to God, Abel's was accepted, Cain's was refused. Each son brought the firstfruits of his vocation as an offering to God. Cain brought from the soil, because that was his lifework. Abel brought from his flocks, because he could bring nothing else. Why Abel's offering was preferred we are not told. One can only speculate. Some of life's conflicts have no simple solutions. It could be that the writer was not interested in that question. Apparently he felt God has a right to some secrets of his own. This is a common plight of the meantime . . . finding the cards stacked against us. We can cry "unfair" all we like, still Cain had to deal with reality, which was this conflict over religion.

Why Cain's offering was refused, we may never know. What we do know, however, is that the writer is extremely interested in spotlighting Cain's anger at God: "So Cain was very angry, and his countenance fell" (v. 5). Cain not only got angry at God but stayed angry. He never got over this incident. The Hebrew reads "it became hot to him." He was so dejected that "his faces fell." Cain, like Lucy in the comic strip, was obviously distressed. Charlie Brown kept coming to her rescue, offering Kool-Aid, a candy bar, a glass of chocolate milk. Then he asked, "Can I do anything else?" Lucy stormed out, "Leave me alone. I just want to be miserable!" That was Cain. He wanted to be miserable. He was hurt. It made him angry and he refused to be comforted.

Cain wasn't the first to cry "Leave me alone!" His parents did it with their fig-leaf aprons. He won't be the last. Job did it. "Leave me alone!" he cried in realistic bitterness (Job 7:16). God is saying to us that there is a mystery in suffering that he hasn't seen fit to reveal yet. But this desire to be left alone forces us to identify with Cain for we must admit that we too get angry at God and sometimes take it out on other people. Cain refused to be comforted because his jealousy so wounded his pride until it permeated every corner of his existence. Hurt pride turned to anger which resulted in suspicion; that suspicion became hatred and this hatred was projected onto brother Abel—the scapegoat! Sometimes we detest what is in us so that we deny it is there and dump on others. Cain couldn't take it out on God so brother Abel would do just fine.

Now this story may be ancient but the feelings it brings to the surface are current. Occasions for hurt pride and anger are numerous for people in transition and how to react to them constructively is one of life's greatest challenges. Cain chose the wrong way. He denied it and projected it. Blinded by his pain, it didn't matter to him that Abel was his brother. He ignored God's warning and his promise. He just wanted to be left alone.

We don't have to live too long until we learn that life won't leave us alone. The Internal Revenue Service won't leave us alone. Our families won't. The church won't; neither will God. He didn't let Sodom alone or Nineveh or Jerusalem or Babylon. The Bible is a record of a God who won't leave us alone. He will bother us when we err. Moses didn't let the Hebrews alone in Egyptian slavery. Nathan the prophet didn't leave King David alone when he callously murdered Uriah the Hittite. "Thou art the man!" thundered the prophet. Elijah didn't let Jezebel alone for stealing Naboth's vineyard. Jesus didn't let Zacchaeus alone, or Peter, or Mary. John the Baptist didn't let Herodias alone for her commitment of adultery.

And God didn't let Cain alone in his agony. "The Lord said to Cain, 'Why are you angry? . . . If you do not do well, sin is couching at the door; its desire is for you, but you must master it' " (Gen. 4:6-7). But Cain didn't heed God's warning. Then God promised his care, "If you do well, will you not be accepted?" (v. 7a). In other words, God is more interested in the way we live than being impressed by sacrifice and ritual. This gives us at least a hint at why Abel's offering was received. Faithful behavior! "Doing well" is what God is after and Cain or anybody else can do well. Cain wouldn't see the open door of acceptance. All he could see was God preferring Abel's offering. Vengeance is an emotional word. And most of us have some appetite for it. It is so natural when we've been wronged; our gut reaction is to retaliate. This primitive response of vengeance is why it's so hard to escape the popular philosophy: "Don't get mad, get even." That slogan has been embodied by many for a long time. It is a result of man's behavior outside the Garden. So Cain killed Abel (v. 8), and like his father and mother before him, set in motion a whole chain of events which he could no longer control. Eden's gate had shut again! The first time God did the shutting. This time Cain did.

In the midst of all the horror movies that come out of Hollywood I was struck by the popular story of Frankenstein. Frankenstein was a student of physiology who constructed a monster and gave it a particular kind of life. The monster turned on his creator and wreaked havoc all around. Today we use the term "Frankenstein monster" to symbolize someone who is destroyed by his own works. It is a fitting model for anyone who uses vengeance. Cain created his own Frankenstein because of mishandled emotions. That was the cause. Now let's look at the cost.

The Cost of Conflict

At last Cain thought he was free of the sheepherder, but God wouldn't leave him alone. God missed Abel. His question must have irked Cain sorely. But he had lost control of the situation, so God stepped in. "Where is Abel your brother?" God asked (v. 9). To protect himself Cain lied, "I do not know." Then he insulted God, sarcastically asking, "Am I my brother's keeper?" Or, "Do I have to shepherd the shepherd?" Cain tried to play innocent but quickly learned that he couldn't fool God. He failed to see that what he did to his brother affected God, too. And although he didn't "keep his brother," God said he *was* "his brother's keeper." We are responsible for what we do.

How nice it would be if we could do like Alan Ladd in the movie *Shane,* and ride off toward the mountains leaving humanity and our responsibility to others behind. Brandon de Wilde ran after him crying, "Shane, Shane, come back Shane." But Shane didn't come back. If we could, we would like to be free of other people. That is the "Cain Syndrome."

But God comes back, "What have you done? The voice of your brother's blood is crying out to me from the ground" (v. 10). God has no place in his world for a person who refuses to be responsible for others. Neither did Jesus who said, "As you did it to one of the least of these . . . you did it to me" (Matt. 25:40). Like a guillotine the consequences of Cain's behavior fell upon his irresponsibility. To farmer Cain God said, "You are cursed from the ground . . . (v. 11). And Cain became a vagabond, "a fugitive and a wanderer" (v. 14).

What was his attitude? Well, Cain just sloughed it off. If that is the way it has to be, then he would just clear out. He didn't have to take anything off anybody—not even God!

But then the loneliness began to gnaw at him. Suppose someone should harm him like he did brother Abel? Cain learned fast that pain is possible to those in transition. He was fair game to all. He came to his moment of truth when he sadly cried, "My punishment is greater than I can bear" (v. 13).

But God still cared for Cain. He persistently dogged him. He wouldn't leave him alone in judgment, now he wouldn't leave him alone in mercy. He promised Cain his protection. God tempered his judgment with mercy, doing for Cain what Cain refused to do for Abel—be his keeper. As a sign of his protection, God put a mark on Cain's forehead (v. 15). The mark is not to be misrepresented as a curse, but a sign of grace, intended for Cain's protection. God is merciful even to a murderer, and that can only be good news for those familiar with failure.

"Then Cain went away from the presence of the Lord, and dwelt in the land of Nod, east of Eden" (v. 16). Nod means "fugitive" or "wandering." Absence from God is the result of Cain's conflict. Cain lived in a constant state of transition and restlessness. Unable to be at home anywhere, he was doomed to wander in vain. The meantime had whipped him.

This is the "way of Cain" mentioned by the writer of Jude (v. 11). By the time of the New Testament days, this sort of behavior had been coined "the way of Cain." It stood for the cynic, skeptic, materialist, who believed neither in God nor moral order in the world. Cain is the epitome of a man who tried to live exactly as he pleased. And those who go the "way of Cain" usually find that living the way we please isn't very pleasing. It was true then and is still true today, the person who chooses to go without God is going to have to reckon with him. Those who go the "way of Cain" will still have to learn, always with pain and sometimes through tragedy, that you can't defy the moral order of God's universe with impunity.

The Cure for Conflict

Honesty will keep us from pointing a blaming finger at Cain. We Nod-dwellers know something of his guilt. We may not be murderers, but we have certainly injured other people by entertaining Cain's philosophy of life . . . living as we please. We know from experience that the cost of conflict is high—so high that we may wonder if there is a cure. There is a cure. It is symbolized by the mark of protection that God put on Cain (v. 15). It stands for grace and mercy. The cure for conflict is bound up in the Second Adam, the One in whom all our pasts can be reconciled. It's all there in the Bible. It begins in Genesis in Nod, east of Eden, and ends up in Revelation with its promise of that great city, the new Jerusalem, descending out of heaven from God (Rev. 2:10), in the midst is a "tree of life," of which "the leaves of the tree were for the healing of the nations" (22:2). In between this Old Testament message from Genesis and the New Testament Book of Revelation is the story of *God's People in Transition.*

Ernest Campbell pinpointed Cain's problem in his book *Locked in a Room with Open Doors.* I bought that book without reading a line of the text. The title really grabbed me. What an image that phrase creates! Campbell suggests that a person can be so immobilized by inner emotions as well as outer obstacles that it's like being in a room with the doors open but still unable to be free. This is where Cain differed from his father. The writer of Genesis portrayed Adam's alienation resulting from the closing of a physical gate. Eden's door was externally locked. Cain's barrier, however, was internal but just as real and certainly a much more effective barrier because it ruined his attitude. Campbell's image rings true. Cain was a prisoner although the doors were open.

The "healing of the nations" could have happened to him if he had heeded God's warning and relied on his mercy. In the later history of the Hebrews we find others who learned Campbell's secret a lot earlier than he did. A pronounced departure from the "way of Cain" occurs in Jeremiah's time when he did not yield to vengeance but left it in the hands of God: "let me see thy vengeance upon them, for to thee have I committed my cause" (Jer. 11:20). The same theme of repudiating vengeance is mentioned in Mark's Gospel relating to Jesus, who was also plotted against, yet he did not retaliate. Francis Bacon said, "By taking revenge, a man is but even with his enemy; but in passing over it, he is superior." Perhaps that was inspired by the life of the Nazarene.

Nevertheless, what they learned, we can too. We can rely on God's mercy. This is the way to cope with conflict in transition or any other time. It is opposite the "way of Cain." It is the way to keep from being "locked in a room with open doors," or from being blinded by hatred, self-pity, or arrogance. It will keep us humble enough to hear and wise enough to heed the voice of God when he reminds us that we *are* our brother's keeper. Whether we go his way toward peace and life or reject it and move toward conflict and death is our choice. Such are the decisions thrust upon us Nod-dwellers in the thick of transition. Our happiness or sorrow to a large extent will depend upon whether the doors of life will become a barrier to block our growth or a passageway to enter on the pilgrimage to fulfillment. Which will it be for you? Jesus said: "I am the door; if any one enters by me, he will be saved, and will go in and out and find pasture" (John 10:9). That is the way that the "children of Cain" can become "sons of God!"

2
Abraham: Faith of a Man on the Move

"Keeping the ball alive," is a phrase coined by sportscasters which describes what happens when a basketball player attempts a rebound and loses control of the ball. In a last ditch effort he will try to deflect the ball against the backboard or tip it in the air, hoping that a teammate can regain control of the ball.

"Keeping the ball alive" is a good way to describe the life of Abraham, Old Testament patriarch, who spent most of his days struggling under the backboard.

By faith Abraham obeyed when he was called to go out to a place which he was to receive as an inheritance; and he went out, not knowing where he was to go. By faith he sojourned in the land of promise, as in a foreign land, living in tents with Isaac and Jacob, heirs with him in the same promise. For he looked forward to the city which has foundations, whose builder and maker is God (Heb. 11:8-11).

Most of his life was an effort to keep his vision alive. He did it by hanging in there . . . which is what this chapter is about, namely, the timeless struggle to keep alive one's vision, faith, and purpose. Keeping the vision alive is compounded by transition, which makes Abraham's struggle all the more relevant to you and me.

Like rungs on a ladder the writer of Genesis 12 triggers our imagination to anticipate what it must have been like for Abraham to launch out from the safety of his homeland to go out into the insecurity of the unknown.

"Now the Lord said to Abram, 'Go . . .'" (v. 1).

29

"So Abram went . . ." (v. 4).

"And Abram journeyed on . . ." (v. 9).

There we have a capsule of a man on the move. But Abraham was more than a mere traveler, a transient who restlessly wandered from one oasis to the next. He was a man with a vision, who worshiped a God who said, "Go," and "he went," and continued to "journey on." Abraham experienced a call from God and responded to it by faith, which led to his struggle with transition. Living in the meantime causes people to grow cautious and afraid of the unknown. We face the danger of operating on the principle of "safety first." But to pattern our lives after him of whom it was said, "God is not ashamed to be called [his] God," necessitates a reckless willingness to adventure. If faith doesn't involve risks, it is not faith. If faith can see each step of the way, it is not faith. It is often necessary for us to step out, trusting God, not knowing what the consequences will be. Perhaps this ancient traveler can be of help to us in such times.

His entire life was characterized by movement and most of the uncertainty was brought on by his religious beliefs. Instead of Abraham's faith being like an anchor to hold during the storms of life, it was more like a full sail. Being a man on the move, Abraham traveled light. He never lived in anything but a tent because he was journeying all his life: from Haran to Canaan; then to Egypt and back to Canaan where he remained, although he never possessed the Promised Land. Instead, he wandered around in it as his offspring was later to wander around in the wilderness. God's promise to Abraham was never fully realized in his lifetime, yet he did not abandon his faith.

Folks like us who are always in a hurry seem to have a harder time waiting than we do with adventure. The hardest part of all is the "time in between." To use Tournier's model of the trapeze—the moment when we are suspended in midair, after letting go of one bar and are reaching out to another. This is the in-between time, when we wait and watch and work and nothing seems to be happening. It is the agony of the meantime that whips so many of us and causes us to sink into apathy. Our dream dies. We lose our vision and our faith. But Abraham was a man who kept his hope alive, even in the gray days when there was nothing to do but wait.

So it is no wonder that such a man came to symbolize many things to his descendants. But there is one that towers above all the rest, namely, Abraham was a man of great faith. At this point both Judaism and Christianity would agree—faith made Abraham what he was. There are several things we can learn from the faith of this man on the move. Time after time when he seemed to come to a dead-end street, Abraham would wait in faith for some further word from the God who started him upon his quest.

God Offers Much but He Also Expects Much (Gen. 17:9)

The first crossroad occurred as Abraham grew older. All he had to go on was a mysterious feeling that God wanted him to come to Canaan. Then came his moment of truth. The time when he knew without a doubt that God was real. "And God said to Abraham, 'As for you, you shall keep my covenant, you and your descendants after you throughout their generations" (Gen. 17:9). God began his communication with a personal word: "As for you." Then he listed the things Abraham must do: keep the covenant himself and teach it to his children. This was a great moment not only for Abraham and the initial action for the makings of a nation; it signaled the truth that people are not complete until they meet God and begin to relate reciprocally. That is what it means to be saved.

Now Abraham was more than just a wanderer. He became a man with a mission. Along with the communication from God came meaning and purpose, both by-products of salvation. In such moments God becomes real when he says to us, "As for you." Now this may sound silly to a society that would rather question God than listen to him, but we must never underestimate anyone who feels God has given him a task to do.

"And I will give to you, and to your descendants after you, the land of your sojournings, all the land of Canaan, for an

everlasting possession; and I will be their God" (Gen. 17:8). God
offered Abraham a lot. But he expected a lot in return. "As for
you." Salvation isn't all gift. It is also demand. God gets around
to the purely personal pronouns and what he said to Abraham
in effect, he says to all; "I will make a covenant with you. You
must keep the covenant and teach it to your children. And I will
be your God." The privileges and obligations go hand in hand.
We must never forget that God says, "As for you," and when
he does, we have to answer.

Abraham Had His Blind Spots (Gen. 15:8)

The next dead end happened when Abraham failed to keep
his part of the covenant. We learn from this that God doesn't
demand us to be perfect before he can use us or work with us.
In my younger days I used to hear people say, "God can't work
in a dirty life." Or "God won't answer sinners' prayers." But
those theories are shot down according to Abraham's life, for
he was anything but perfect. Yet God never quit working with
him. God took Abraham where he was, mixed-up, wavering
back and forth between faith and doubt, and slowly moved him
forward. We see it in his perplexing question: "How am I to
know?" (Gen. 15:8). On several occasions Abraham must have
asked this question. It just reeks of doubt. One such time certainly must have been during his movement from Ur to Palestine when a famine arose. Abraham quit trusting God and
panicked, rushing down to Egypt where food was more plenti-
ful. While he was there living with that question, he sacrificed
his wife to the Egyptians. Admittedly this sacrifice isn't as
popular or sublime as the one on Mt. Moriah where he offered
his son Isaac, but it was a sacrifice just the same. Let me para-
phrase: "Sarah, I understand old Pharaoh is quite a ladies' man
and you are a very attractive woman. Now look, if Pharaoh
takes a liking to you, why don't you just say you're my sister.
Then Pharaoh will show us favor" (Gen. 12:10-19).

Abraham was not perfect. More than once he must have
struggled with that question. He was not perfect when God

called him out of Haran, or during his wandering, or at the end, but God worked with him nonetheless. Abraham had his blind spots and from his lying and bribery we discover that perfection is not a requirement for God to deal with us. It's an encouragement to me to know that this great hero of faith had his moments of bewilderment. If Abraham can cry "How can I know?" and if Jesus can cry, "My God, my God, why have you forsaken me?" then we must make room in our faith for doubt, weakness, and discouragement as well as certainty, hope, and victory. Genuine faith is no fair-weather friend. It is no neat collection of easy answers, rather it is a firm hand placed on the shoulder, urging us out into the unknown future.

In the New Testament, one of Jesus' disciples named Thomas also struggled with the problem of knowledge and faith in his dialogue with Jesus in John 14. Jesus stated that the disciples know "the way where I am going" (v. 4). Thomas came back with the fact that they didn't know and was bold enough to ask, "How can we know . . . ?" (v. 5). Jesus responded, "If you had known me, you would have known my father also" (v. 7). This exchange shows us what can and needs to be known in the area of faith and doubt. How can we know? We can know God. The proof comes in the venture. Jesus spoke of it as a "way."

But Abraham learned what we must all learn—there are no shortcuts to maturity. How can I know? How can I be sure? The answer is, you can't know, but God can, and you must live your life of faith in him. We have to be ready to start where we are and move step by step with faith in God to keep working with us along the way, in spite of our blind spots.

Abraham Accepted What He Could Not Understand (Gen. 22:14)

The third eye-opener for Abraham was when he felt God wanted him to sacrifice his son Isaac. Then he was faced with a situation that is familiar to all of us—when life makes no sense. He had a firm promise from God that he was to have many descendants through which God would bless all the peo-

ple of the earth. Finally, after a long interim, the son of promise
came in Abraham and Sarah's old age. Through Isaac would this
promise be fulfilled. The whole thing hinged on Isaac and now
Abraham thought God wanted to take that life away. "God
tested Abraham, and said to him, . . . 'Take your son, your only
son Isaac, whom you love, and go to the land of Moriah, and
offer him there as a burnt offering' " (Gen. 22:1-2). We have no
trouble identifying with Abraham here. Into every life comes
those occasions when life makes no sense. Things happen and
we are left to grope for reasons to make sense out of it all and
we come up empty.

Surely this is how John the Baptist felt in prison when he had
dedicated his life to preparing the way for the Messiah and yet,
the Messiah didn't seem to be doing things the way he predict-
ed it would happen. So he echoed Abraham's question, "Are
you he who is to come, or shall we look for another?" (Matt.
11:3). It is in such moments that we are faced with one of life's
hardest battles—the struggle to accept that which we cannot
understand. In such times there is only one thing to do—accept
it and trust God to do what's right. This is what John did. It is
what Jesus did: "Into thy hands I commit my spirit." It is what
Abraham did. We see it when little Isaac said, "Behold, the fire
and the wood, but where is the lamb for a burnt offering?" Then
comes a word painted with faith and heartbreak at the same
time: "God will provide." It's almost sacrilegious to say anything further, but I am compelled to point out that the real
revelation of God came in verse 12 (Gen. 22): "Do not lay your
hand on the lad or do anything to him." God provided a ram
in the thicket.

The real revelation was when God *stopped* Abraham from
thrusting the knife through Isaac's heart. But the point is, when
life no longer made any sense, Abraham obeyed anyway. The
best always results when we do that. This story is more than
an attempt to explain why the Hebrew faith, alone in the ancient world, rejected child sacrifice. It is a symbol of holy
ground, a place where radical obedience to God and deep reli-

gious faith was implemented. Abraham learned a lot about God that day because he trusted him with everything he had. Like Jesus who later praised a poor widow who dropped her last two pennies in the offering, Abraham gave all he had. Isaac was it. He was his only son and the promise depended upon him. Just so, we can never know much about God until we trust him with everything. Trust him a little and you'll know him a little. Job said, "Though he slay me, yet will I trust him." He knew "God would provide." The widow knew it. And those disciples knew it that Palm Sunday when they were told to go get a young donkey and bring it to Jesus. If anyone questioned it, they were told to say, "The master needs it." Strange instructions obeyed anyway. They didn't understand anymore than Abraham did, but they still got the donkey. Sometimes faith and obedience pull rank over logic. Sometimes you do things although you don't know why, other than Jesus tells you to do it. The disciples did it because they recognized his claim on them and they knew what Abraham knew, "God would provide!" And he did. And he will.

Abraham Never Went Back (Gen. 24:8)

The last episode occurred when Abraham was on his death-bed and the burning issue on his mind was the covenant God made with him. Abraham had taken the plunge long ago in Haran when he left the land of his people. He went, not knowing what lay ahead but felt that God would guide him. He had known great hardship along the way, but there were rewards. Abraham felt the wrath of God when he disobeyed and mercy when he was faithful. During the meantime, it was the covenant that kept him going. When he was ready to die, Abraham wanted to get a wife for Isaac so he could have children to carry on the covenant. To do this, he called in his most trusted servant and instructed him to return to Haran, the place of his kin, and choose a wife for Isaac. But he gave him one clear warning: "See to it that you do not take my son back there" (v. 6). And again for emphasis: "You must not take my son back there" (v.

8). The intention, I believe, is "Never allow Isaac to return to Haran, the land of my people. No matter what happens, he must not go back." It's incredible to me that Abraham could maintain this stance about his homeland. Perhaps the people may tempt Isaac to stay and not possess the promise. But Abraham never seemed to be homesick like his descendants, when they wandered around in the desert, yearning for the fleshpots of Egypt. Maybe Abraham remembered the tragedy that happened to Lot's wife when she looked back. No matter. Abraham never did. What he began, he finished and persevered to the end. One of the problems of our day is we turn back too soon. We have fantastic starting power, but we lack staying power. So Abraham warned, "You must not go back. Under no circumstances are you to take Isaac back to Haran."

How was he able to have this attitude? Perhaps it was because of the pull of the promise that enabled him to burn his bridges. Life to Abraham was not back in Haran. It was out there on into the unknown future—that's where the vision was leading.

The lesson of Abraham's life is we have to put our past in proper perspective. Yes, it is an inescapable part of our lives. Yes, we should learn as much as we can from it. But we must never retreat to the past. There is a world of difference between reclaiming the past and living in it. Haran is a part of all of us, but our vision lies out ahead. Our hope is in him who calls us forth just as he did Abraham, and proposes a covenant and guides the faithful with his purpose and strength.

"You must not go back!" This is what we have to keep in mind when transition creates unrest and uncertainty and so much change all around us. We are often tempted to find relief from the tension by retreating to our particular Harans, where we were secure and stable and life was simple. And many fall into this trap. But we must not go back to the old ways of life or thought. We must go forward in faith.

The modern sport of skydiving illustrates well the sort of faith we must have. Can you imagine what it would be like to leap out of an airplane five thousand feet above the ground and free-fall at speeds of over 120 miles per hour, and then wait until you are close to the earth to pull the ripcord? Now that calls for faith. It calls for faith that the parachute will open when it's supposed to. It calls for trust. A skydiver never knows the thrill of the sport until he jumps out of the airplane. Even so, one never knows the power of God to provide until he or she steps out in trust and commits his life to God. Once you've jumped out of the plane you can't go back.

Haran has a lot going for it. But the person called of God to move out and face the future of change can never go back. Yes, Abraham would admit his indebtedness to Haran, that's where he got his start. But he will still firmly insist, "we must never go back," but keep faith with the vision and keep it alive by answering God's call and obeying his covenant, facing life feetfirst, confident in the future because we serve a God who says "Go!" If we go, he'll be with us.

Go therefore and make disciples of all nations, baptizing them in the name of the Father and of the Son and of the Holy Spirit, teaching them to observe all that I have commanded you; and lo, I am with you always, to the close of the age (Matt. 28:19-20).

That is the vision. Will you keep it alive? You can do it with faith!

3
Joseph: Learning to Live with Pain

In a contemporary novel is a devastating exposé of professional football. It has been made into an intriguing film about an aging tight-end who learned to play football with pain. Betraying blatant greed as a prime motivator behind the sport, the athlete's disdain for his body is outdone only by the owners, who treat players like "equipment." What the big business of professional football did to his body is not nearly as serious as what it did to his spirit. The football player is convincing when he confesses that life's greatest glory comes when he catches a pass. That is his god. He would endure most anything to get that "high." The story is an interesting study in the quest for meaning in life and the things people will endure to achieve it.

Living with pain is a fitting model of the life of Joseph, favorite son of Jacob, whose pain came from the hard knocks of life rather than a football game. Joseph's life portrayed in Genesis 37—50 provides an interesting contrast to the tight-end because he found meaning in the midst of pain in a way that is much more fulfilling than the dehumanizing life of the professional athlete.

If a man is what he proves to be in an emergency, then we have ample material to find out what Joseph was made of. Like the football player he too struggled with circumstances that were beyond his control. Like salvo blasts from a huge cannon Joseph endured three terrible injustices that were set in motion the moment he found himself in the midst of transition. Being uprooted from his homeland against his will and sold into slav-

ery and taken to Egypt where he was a stranger, Joseph somehow was able to face these injustices of life by learning to live
with pain. He has much to teach us about coping with the
meantime.

Joseph was a dreamer. But he did what he could to make his
dreams come true. He was loved very much by his father, Jacob,
because he was the oldest son of his favorite wife, Rachel. But
because Joseph was loved as a child he learned to handle himself well in the face of trouble.

His brothers, however, reacted in jealousy at Jacob's favorit-
ism and became hostile toward Joseph. Joseph's brothers
teamed up against him because of their anger at Jacob and their
resentment of Joseph's dreams about them "bowing down" to
him.

Unwittingly Jacob thrust his son into this seething cauldron
of hostility one day when he sent Joseph to check on his brothers tending the flocks in a place called Dothan. Joseph was
mature enough to follow these difficult orders without complaining. So he left his father, never to see him again for many
years. Before he arrived, his brothers conspired against him.

Sure enough, Joseph discovered that obeying his father was
the pits! For that's exactly where he ended up—in a hole in the
ground. He was attacked by his own flesh and blood, the famous coat given to him as a symbol of his father's love was
ripped to shreds, and he was held captive. Outside, he could
hear them plotting to kill him but Judah came up with a better
idea. Why not sell him and make a profit in the meantime?
Which they did. Joseph was treated like "equipment" but at
least he was alive, even if he was a slave. His brothers callously
sold him for twenty pieces of silver to a band of Midianite
traders who took him down to Egypt to be sold there for even
more profit. Like the comic strip "Ziggy," Joseph records these
experiences in his diary: "Dear Diary, Today was lots better
than yesterday. I only had eight minor mishaps, three temporary setbacks, and four disappointments. Then after breakfast.
. . ." Joseph had had better days. But being spared from death

at the hands of his brothers, now he was a slave and only swapped one form of death for another.

Thus, Joseph's transition began in a pit in Dothan and ended up on a throne in Egypt. But in between these two events was a lot of pain. Up to this time Joseph had been sheltered by his father, constantly being by his side. Almost abruptly he met his first ambush and he responded well. Joseph must have asked, "What will I do in response to circumstances beyond my control?" Joseph did four things in response to the life of hard knocks and learned to live with the pain by persevering in the face of injustice. Joseph discovered early in life that bad things happen to the upright. Life holds the potential for the absurd and the meaningless. Joseph faced a future of loneliness and pain and I'm sure on more than one occasion he thought, *What's the use?* Instead he learned to live with pain. Let's see how.

1. *He rolled with the punches.*—"The Lord was with Joseph" (Gen. 39:2).

First, Joseph developed the ability to roll with the punches from life. He didn't need a routine in order to be secure because he learned to cope with change effectively. Some people need to have things structured and ordered or they go to pieces with any change in their circumstances, but not Joseph. Separated from the security of his father and his familiar surroundings, he was a stranger in a foreign country. That was quite a step down from favorite son to common slave. I'm sure there are many refugees that could identify with Joseph, but what about us? How would you respond in such a situation?

A person who rolls with the punches may wince from the pain, but he keeps on living in spite of it. The tight-end in the novel relied on pain-killing drugs to play football with his pain. But that didn't kill the pain. It only postponed it, meanwhile doing greater damage to his injured knee. Joseph had no morphine or other miracle painkillers. He just did the best he could with what he had in the situation. Thus, he set out to try to make his dreams come true. In the process, he suffered from this jolt. But he didn't let it turn him sour.

Perhaps Joseph was able to maintain this attitude because of the presence of God in his life (v. 2). God was with Joseph! He was with him in the pit, he was with him in the slave train with the Midianites, and he was with Joseph down in Egypt where he was bought by an Egyptian official named Potiphar.

Thus, Joseph continued doing what he could with what he had and became productive and useful to his owner. He obviously set some realiable goals and set out to reach them. He worked hard. His integrity, industriousness, and sharp mind set him apart from all the rest of Potiphar's apathetic slaves. So Joseph naturally advanced quickly. It wasn't long before he was entrusted with the special responsibility of managing Potiphar's household. Doing what he could with what he had was Joseph's way of rolling with the punches instead of bristling against them. And up to this point he was doing all right.

2. *He knew how to say no.*—"How then can I do this great wickedness?" (Gen. 39:9).

But if Potiphar believed Joseph was interesting, his wife felt even more so. Apparently Joseph was a good-looking young man. Potiphar's wife tried to seduce him openly. "Lie with me," she said bluntly. Imagine the stress this put on Joseph! Surely his blood was as red as the next man's, and he was torn between his humanness, his loyalty to Potiphar, and the seductiveness of Potiphar's wife. Yet, Joseph again responded nobly, for he had the wisdom to say no.

Why not? a voice entices. *Just this once. Besides, everybody else is doing it. And she did ask me. I'm away from home and nobody knows me. When in Egypt, do as the Egyptians do. After all, she's lonely too, plus it may even advance my career."* But no!

No is the hardest word for any of us to learn to say. Joseph said it by refusing to break his trust with Potiphar. He had the commitment and the courage to say no. People involved with transition are going to need this word often. For many kinds of situations will arise which seem to be attractive on the surface, but lurking down below is the ugliness of sin. Many would accept every invitation to keep from offending others. But Joseph knew how to say no when he ought to say no. And he had the guts to say it. The same opportunity probably presents itself thousands of times to folks on the move—only the names are different. Modern-day Josephs are asked, "Why not?" One is lonely, the other is willing. "Why not?" But Joseph counters with this: My master has not "kept anything from me except yourself, because you are his wife; how then can I do this great wickedness, and sin against God?" (v. 9).

Obviously Joseph felt he was accountable to God for his actions. Because God was with him, Joseph felt accountable. To Joseph, cheating with another man's wife was a sin, not merely "sowing wild oats." "How can I do this great wickedness, and sin against God?" When we recognize that God is present in our lives, we will put boundaries on ourselves. Because God was present, Joseph didn't feel right doing as he pleased. So he rejected the opportunity. Joseph knew that sex is a gift from God, and it can only be mutually beneficial when lovers are committed to each other in the bonds of marriage. He was accountable to God.

Joseph was also accountable to Potiphar. Personal integrity demanded that he not break the confidence of his owner. Nor would he cheaply exploit another man's wife, no matter how willing she was. He who was treated like equipment refused to take advantage of either Potiphar or his wife. Thus, he avoided being squeezed into a vise of personal conflict. At least he thought he had. But Potiphar's wife turned on Joseph with all the fury of her lust, only this time framing him in front of her husband by lying and making it look like Joseph was trying to rape her. The result of Joseph's saying no? Back to the pits! Potiphar had him thrown in prison. Who would believe a foreign slave against the testimony of one's wife? Bad things continue to happen to those who are responsible. There is no guarantee that good behavior will ward off injustice, so Joseph was in the pits again . . . the result of a second raw deal beyond his control.

3. *He channeled negative feelings into positive use.*—"God sent me before you to preserve for you a remnant on earth, and to keep alive for you many survivors" (Gen. 45:7).

But, because Joseph learned to roll with the punches and live with pain, Joseph didn't let this injustice destroy him. He didn't complain or blame God. No doubt he was angry, and rightly so, but unlike his ancestor Cain, he didn't let his anger get the best of him by causing him to do something he would be sorry for later on. Instead, Joseph turned right where Cain and his brothers turned wrong—he channeled his negative feelings into positive uses. Joseph took advantage of the time on his hands, thirteen years to be exact. Again, making the best of a bad situation—he did what he could and soon became productive, even in prison. He was placed in charge of all the other prisoners because he relied on his gift as a dreamer and became friends with two men close to Pharaoh. One was later released and Joseph had a thread of hope. However, the servant promptly forgot the dreamer from Palestine. That's the way life is sometimes. People will forget about you when you need them. Injustice again! Still Joseph persevered. "But the Lord was with Joseph and showed him steadfast love" (v. 21).

While God was with Joseph, Pharaoh was having some bothersome dreams that he couldn't understand. Neither could anyone else. Pharaoh needed a dreamer and—snap—the servant remembered Joseph. He was raised from the pits again! Interpreting Pharaoh's dream, Joseph warned him of a famine coming to Egypt. And Pharaoh was so impressed with Joseph that he promoted the young Hebrew to second in command in all of Egypt. His task was to prepare for the famine. Sure enough, famine came and all the neighboring people came to buy grain from Joseph. It was learning to live with pain by channeling his negative emotions into constructive uses that led the way out of the pits again. It also paved the way for one final response from Joseph that showed what he was really made of.

4. *Joseph held no grudges.*—"As for you, you meant evil against me; but God meant it for good" (Gen. 50:20).

The famine opened the door for Joseph to be reunited with his family. His brothers came to Egypt in search of food, totally unaware that Joseph was "back in control." He made his dreams come true. There were his brothers bowing before the one they had previously sold into slavery. But Joseph held no grudges because he loved his brothers and had compassion on them. Breaking into tears at the sight of them, he ran out of the room before they could learn who he was. Joseph wasn't afraid to feel because he had felt a lot of pain and he learned to live with pain which could be one reason why he held no grudges. Joseph didn't rely on painkillers but, in every injustice, felt and owned his pain.

Joseph forgave his brothers for their ghastly act. By this time Joseph had absorbed several hard knocks from life, and rather than turn bitter, he grew better. If Joseph had anything, it was a healthy self-image. Revealing his identity to his brothers wasn't done in a grandiose manner, bragging about his accomplishments. He never said, "Look how great I am!" He simply said, "I am Joseph" (45:3). Here was a man in touch with himself. This revelation terrified his brothers. But the brothers were quickly relieved when Joseph asked about his father. "I am Joseph; is my father still alive?" It became obvious that he was more concerned about family ties than revenge. He used his power unselfishly, not to get even, but to feed hungry people.

By this time Joseph was spiritually mature. He had developed a close relationship with God and this afforded him the opportunity to maintain vast power and control over others but at the same time keep his wealth, fame, and exaltation in proper perspective. He didn't sell his soul "for a mess of pottage," like his ancestor, Esau. Joseph used power to glorify God and serve mankind. A person who knows how God uses power will never surrender his soul to it; and, if he can't put it to positive uses, he will reject it outright. We don't know when Joseph learned this important lesson. But, if the "pits" had anything to do with his learning the lesson, we ought to find out how to get there and spend a little time in the pits ourselves. The things Joseph kept in proper perspective are the very things that we transients worship to our grave. Love of money, worship of pleasure and ease, a search for security at all costs—these are the real gods in the lives of so many on the move. We do not want to live with pain. It must be avoided at all costs. Like a young girl on the recent TV special entitled "Angel Dust," describing her reasons for using PCP: "I can't stand the pain, man. So I get high." In the process of devoting our lives to these gods unworthy of our worship, we also forfeit our souls to them. Our society has taught us to measure our success by competition. We determine our greatness by the number of our brothers who bow down before us. Very few are aware of the lesson Joseph learned from the pits; namely, we need other people as brothers and sisters, not as slaves to bow down before us.

And although Joseph needed his brothers, he didn't let them off cheaply. "Come near to me, I pray you," and they came near. And he said, "I am your brother, Joseph, whom you sold into Egypt" (v. 4). Many would have never mentioned this unpleasant memory. But Joseph was firm and reminded them of their betrayal because he felt they were accountable to him for what they did. Vengeance wasn't his motive because he was willing to forgive. "Do not be distressed, or angry with yourselves, because you sold me here; for God sent me before you to preserve life" (v. 5). Joseph held no grudges because of his relationship with God. God was with Joseph and used all these hard knocks to provide food for starving people during the famine. "That's why I'm here today," Joseph told his brothers, "and that's why I forgive you." Only a man with deep faith could maintain such perseverance in the face of gross injustice. Joseph had the patience to wait on God to make things right, and in his own good time, God did.

Summary

What can we learn from Joseph's struggles in his transition from the pit to the throne? I can think of two main ideas:

1. Virtue doesn't pay off immediately. One of the difficult facts of life is that when we choose the evil, we get what we want immediately. Then we pay for it afterward. But when we choose the good as Joseph did, we often have to pay for it first, before we get it. Why the world was made like that, I don't know. I just know it is. Like the oil-filter commercial where the man says, "Pay me now or pay me later." This immediate gratification leans in evil's favor. This is especially a subtle temptation with our credit-card culture. Take it, never mind about the bills. They will come in later. Take what you want now. The quick, easy, and often dishonest choices of life often present immediate gains. But the noble decisions, the long-term aims that make for strong character, intelligence, and service have to be paid for first. We pay for devotion and self-discipline in advance. We must not be fooled by the subtlety of evil here. Especially in a time of transition we may be susceptible to purchasing immediate desires on the installment plan. But rest assured that the bills do come in! When Joseph's brothers sold him into slavery, they got twenty pieces of silver immediately. Then they fabricated a lie about a wild animal killing Joseph. This lie broke their father's heart. That's the way it often is when the bills start coming in. Rarely do you alone pay for your wrong. Often you hurt those you never intend to hurt. Others have to pay too. For God's sake, don't run up bills like that . . . which years and years of payments by your family cannot satisfy.

But Joseph wasn't the first and he won't be the last to learn that being a responsible person can lead to raw deals. Trusting God is no guarantee that tragedy won't come. Joseph was thrown into the pit and sold into slavery because he obeyed his earthly father. He was imprisoned in Egypt for thirteen years because he obeyed his heavenly father. Sometimes it seems like there is no justice in this world no matter whom you obey.

Nevertheless, virtue doesn't pay off immediately. We set ourselves up for disappointment when we expect it to do so.

2. What a person does to life is more than what life does to
a person. What life does to us depends on what life finds in us.
What happens to us externally doesn't determine the consequence. External circumstances merely pull the trigger which
explodes us. The consequence depends on what was in us to
explode. Joseph didn't explode because he took the presence of
God seriously in his life. That soft-spoken slogan, almost unno-
ticed but never forgotten, flashes throughout Joseph's interim:
"The Lord was with Joseph." And because God is who he is,
there is always something that can be done when life gives us
a raw deal. Here is the key to Joseph's secret—although he
didn't *find* life worth living, he *made* it worth living. And all
others who do the same do it the way he did, namely, by
internal spiritual perseverance. This is an important truth in the
face of life's impartiality. The Preacher in Ecclesiastes, the most
pessimistic author in the Old Testament, knew of the impartiality of life. "Everything before them is vanity, since one fate
comes to all, to the righteous and the wicked, to the good and
the evil . . . as is the good man, so is the sinner" (Eccl. 9:1-2).
So it appears. For awhile, at least, it looked like that in Joseph's
case. Birth and death, joy and sorrow, sickness and health, love
and loss, happiness and tragedy—they are no respecter of persons.

The Preacher is right in one sense. On Calvary three crosses
stood. On one side was a blasphemous thief; a repentant thief
on the other. The Christ was in the middle. Life is impartial.
This world isn't run right, some may say. When a hurricane
wrecks a town, it levels churches and schools as well as beer
joints and brothels. Life is impartial. But is it now? Joseph
evidently knew a secret, later pointed out by Jesus in his parable
of the two men who built houses, one on the sand and the other
on a solid rock. The same things happened to both alike. The
rain fell, floods descended, and the winds blew. After the storm
was over, one house was gone and one house was left standing.

The difference depended upon the foundations of the houses. And in an emergency as no other time we see what people are made of. There's no doubt what Joseph was made of. Some people go to pieces and others have a strong persistent faith. But the final outcome depends on the foundation of our lives.

Embellishing on the great Christian doctrine of the resurrection, one saint said: "The church worships a God who knows his way out of the grave!" Jesus of Nazareth showed us that you can't bury him permanently. Yes, you can hurt him—even kill him, but Jesus came forth from the tomb and it was a persistent faith in that kind of God which enabled Joseph to endure the worst that life could do and still be pulled up out of the depths of injustice of the pits and prisons of this world.

Like one of God's other jailbirds who wrote: "I can do all things in him who strengthens me" (Phil 4:13). If Paul could and Joseph could, so can we. It depends on what we're made of. It depends on whether we are hollow on the inside or full of the faith that enables us to persevere in the face of injustice because we know we serve a God who "knows his way out of the grave!" If we believe that, then we too can learn to live with pain.

4
Moses: Enduring the Detours of Life

An interesting fact about the popular movie *American Graffiti* is that it features the music of the sixties with a theme based on the fifties, but was produced in the seventies. Truly, it was a multi-generational picture and my hunch is that it was popular because of the common thread of movement. Cars were constantly in motion, cruising after dark up and down the boulevards and the dragstrips. Folks of these three decades have been on the move. And the direction we are going is affected by the way we interpret what happens to us along the way. Another theme of the movie was that the kids seemed to be getting nowhere in their search for meaning. Several were coming face to face with life's detours.

The film raised a good question—how do we interpret the detours of life? Our perception of the detours and our response to them has a powerful impact upon the direction in which we move.

In a more positive vein, Carol Burnette's daughter was featured in *People* magazine because she was learning to cope with what now has become a common detour in the form of drug abuse. The teenager decided to meet her problem head-on, deal with it constructively. She entered a program for drug abuse and experienced pain for awhile, then she set out to perceive a new course, a new pattern, and a different use of the scattered pieces of her problem. Life's detours can have that kind of outcome. Wayne Oates makes this same point in his book, *Life's Detours:*

Life's fixed organizations, dreams, hopes, and fantasies have a way of slamming into walls and being smashed. A new way through, over, under, around, or out has to be found. The steadfast resolve under God to find that way results in a detour.[1]

When we slam into the wall, God comes in and takes the pieces of the mess we've made of life and reveals new avenues of opportunity, growth, and hope.

An excellent model for life's detours in biblical perspective is the life of Moses. His struggle with transition began down in Egypt but ended up on Mount Nebo, overlooking "Jordan's stormy banks" and the Promised Land of Canaan. In between, Moses endured a lifelong detour of wandering around in the wilderness.

It all started down in Egypt with a pharaoh inheriting the throne "who knew not Joseph." This resulted in the enslavement of the Hebrew people.

Moses, being a Hebrew, was moved deeply by the mistreatment of his kin. His first reaction was a bad one. Using the method of violence, he killed an Egyptian guard and was forced to flee for his life. Thus, in exile, he laid low for forty years and became a shepherd adopting the more pastoral life of the wilderness.

But God was using Moses' self-imposed exile to prepare a new way to intervene on behalf of his people. He had plans for Moses because the detour in the wilderness greatly mellowed his concept of leadership. The interim between his killing the Egyptian and the burning-bush experience taught Moses a lot about the way God works in our lives. He learned that God is a God of alternatives and that he is persistent in his working with humanity. God does not quit on us as quickly as we give up on ourselves or each other.

Oates points out in his book that there are several laws that can be discovered from the detours of life. I'd like to name a few that are evident in Moses' detour in hopes that it will be of help to people today in similar circumstances.

First, is the law of compensation. This can best be explained in medical terminology. For instance, when a person has to have one kidney removed, the other one will be strengthened to take over the function of the lost kidney. Just so, Oates claims we can use the negative experiences of life creatively and compensate for our loss by turning our detours into positive uses. Moses observed the "law of compensation" during his wilderness exile by mellowing, thus, becoming more fit as a leader of the Hebrews than when he relied on violence during the impatient period of his youth.

All this is amazing when you consider the fact that Moses could have lived on easy street all his days as the adopted son of Pharaoh's daughter. Moses had a choice—to make the world a better place or make a better place for himself in the world. Moses chose the former. He rejected a life of ease and comfort by aligning himself with the downtrodden, making the burdens of his people his own burdens. This pattern was operative in Jesus of Nazareth, who also gave up his glory to identify with a people in need of liberation. He was despised and rejected, but Moses, many years before, shared in the sufferings that Jesus was to endure. A choice was made early in life. Moses decided to cast his loyalty with his own people—a choice which led to suffering and anxiety and hardship, rather than the ease of Egyptian royalty. He would rather suffer for God than enjoy the luxury with those doing wrong.

And all this talk of suffering and loyalty must sound strange to people who live in a time of declining Christian loyalty. Where does our zeal go? Why do most of us resort to the past tense in talking of our service to God? We enact a vicious cycle. First a need arises from some desperate situation. Then after a struggle, people begin to pull together and prosperity occurs. And it's not long before commitment begins to fade again. Gone again! This is our pattern.

Jesse Jackson, minister and social activist, has captured a good model for loyalty and commitment. Devising a formula for improving minority education which he calls "Operation PUSH," he came up with ten commandments, similar to

Moses'. I'd like to mention only number nine: "The practice of convenience leads to collapse, but the laws of sacrifice lead to greatness." Do you sense the loyalty and commitment inherent in that rule? I'm sure Moses wouldn't have had any trouble with it, for he did not choose the soft life of convenience and comfort. Rather it was the sacrificial route that led to suffering but by observing the law of compensation, Moses showed what we can all do during a detour. One thing we can't do is wait around, ignore injustice, and hope that things will get better. That is a decision for the soft life. We must commit ourselves to something and make things get better.

Such was Moses' response—the law of compensation. He committed himself, his time, and his resources; something good always comes from that.

Next, Oates mentions the law of fellowship. One of the outstanding characteristics of Moses was his intimacy with God. Moses relied on his fellowship with God during his detour, which was a big portion of his success. He went into the tabernacle, and the Lord spoke to Moses face to face, as a man speaks to a friend (see Ex. 33:9-11). This was the key to Moses' faith—he knew God intimately. Moses was the kind of man he was because he knew God the way he did. And what Moses did, we can do. Everything he did was a result of coming from the presence of God.

He left the Sinai desert to go into Egypt to liberate the Hebrews because he had met God in the burning-bush experience. He led the children of Israel across the Red Sea because God was with him. God's presence in the wilderness with the transients was symbolized by a cloud by day and a pillar of fire by night. Before coming down from the mountain with the Ten Commandments, Moses was alone in fellowship with God! And when we set out to accomplish a task, having come straight from the presence and intimate fellowship with God, no detour need ever defeat us. Our failure is due to the fact that so often we try to go it alone and forget about fellowship with God or anybody else. We ignore the power of prayer and reject the fellowship of the church. But Moses faced God before he faced Pharaoh and he came away victorious in his mission of liberation.

Our problem is most of us really don't want intimacy with God. We're far more interested in all the gusto we can get. We're too busy searching for the comfortable life to be intimate with anybody, much less God. We don't need fellowship because the carefree life with no moral restraints is so appealing to us. A good example of this was a movie where one of the actors said, "I see what I want and go after it." Well, one of the things she wanted happened to be a happily married man—and she went for him and he went for her. Such people certainly don't want to be intimate with God. For to do so would cramp their style.

Imagine approaching the man in the movie and his lover echoing the prophet Micah's message: "What does the Lord require of you but to do justice, and to love kindness, and to walk humbly with your God?" (6:8). Do justly? No, she saw what she wanted and went after it. She doesn't want God. The philosophy is plain and popular: the universe is nonmoral, the problem of life is to discover what you can get away with in order to be comfortable! A close relationship with God is the last thing the "seducers" of life want. Intimacy with him would surely disrupt their philosophy.

But I have real problems with life's seducers, for nobody "gets away with anything" in God's world. Sooner or later we're all going to have to deal with: "Whatsoever a man sows, that shall he also reap" (Gal. 6:7). Like Cain, we learn that lesson the hard way. And like Jonah, we long to get away from God. We prefer distance to intimacy with him. The less he knows about us the better, and the less we know about him, the more we can seduce others. So we run down to Tarshish to flee the presence of the Lord. We don't want God. We don't want him to redeem Nineveh. We don't care about delivering people who are being mistreated; we just want to be comfortable! I believe it was St. Augustine who prayed: "God grant me chastity, but not yet!" Moses' greatness came because he wanted to be close to God.

I have valued the presence of God the most when a chosen way of life seemed barred and I had to look for another way. For the first twenty years of my life, I wanted to be an athletic coach. However, being small-boned and weak-kneed, my body just wasn't suited for college athletics. Consequently, I spent a lot of time on the operating table . . . a result of "seeing what I wanted and going after it." Finally, after a dislocated hip, a broken collarbone, and knee surgery twice, I decided to hang it up. My first detour! It was then that fellowship became crucial to me. Like the Skylab experiment which went awry, tragedy was diverted because NASA maintained some form of ground control. Such a support system is necessary in life to prevent tragedy. The fellowship of Christian people in my church in South Carolina, the acceptance of a support community was a lifesaver during this detour of life. My burdens were borne before I was able to bear another's burdens. When I had concerned friends caring for me, I knew somehow that God cared too. One of the dangers of a detour is the likelihood of losing our way. But the beauty of Christian fellowship is that there are others available to be guides in our wilderness. Thus, the importance of the law of fellowship during a detour.

Last, Oates speaks of the law of resurrection. The resurrection of Jesus Christ is the bedrock of the Christian faith. He endured many a detour but his life was built on the conviction that though he was crucified, he would rise again. Paul saw this as one of the basic laws of life, "we are being killed all the day long," he said. Thus, the resurrection is a basic law of life and is especially helpful to keep in mind during a detour. We are constantly saying hello and goodbye all our lives. We part and we meet. We come and we go. We move to a place for awhile and we're gone again. And lost people need to find their way. It happens when an old life dies and a new one is born. This is the law of resurrection.

Breaking Away was a beautiful film portraying the idealism of youth and how shattered we become when our idols betray us. One young man became so enthralled with Italian cyclists that he began to eat Italian food, speak the Italian language, and pretend he was a romantic Italian himself. He lived for the day when his heroes would come to Bloomington, Indiana, for the big race. Of course, he entered the race himself and was doing too well. He was far ahead of the Italians. So, when they got close enough, one of them jammed a tire pump into the spokes of his rear wheel, throwing him to the shoulder of the road in an accident. His idols had betrayed him! When that happens and the way of life built around these idols collapses, we fall to the ground and our vision dies. Jesus said we could expect this: "Unless a grain of wheat falls into the earth and dies, it remains alone" (John 12:24). The detours of life are sometimes initiated by such deadends. There is nothing left to do but put it in reverse, back out, and start all over again. But the end of one direction can be the birth of a new one. The young cyclist eventually became the star representing a local group of "cutters" and won the next big race against overwhelming odds. This is the law of resurrection.

Moses knew about it. Jeremiah said, "The people . . . found grace in the wilderness" (Jer. 31:2). Finding grace on a detour of life is no mean task. A detour is a dreary process. It is time consuming, hard, and we face the prospect of getting lost. It is no easy road, but grace can be found in unlikely places. Moses found God in the wilderness. "The place whereon you stand is holy ground!" To find God in such times calls for special insight, which might be helpful to those on detours.

How do we find grace in the wilderness? Moses found it over his indignation against his people being treated like animals. He found it by his loyalty and dedication to liberate them. Moses found his vocation in the wilderness. Now, in our high moments when life is rosy, it's easy to find God. We enter an awesome church where love, beauty, and goodness are present. In such times it is not difficult to find God. But when we're faced with a detour, struggling with the anxiety of transition and all things holy are absent, we lose all sense of God. Where has God gone, we ask? It's in such situations that we need to hear from the God who encountered Moses in the wilderness—an unlikely place.

But now that I think about it, some of the most memorable encounters with God in history have been like that. Moses and God in the desert of Sinai. Elijah and God by the brook. Jonah and God in the belly of a great fish. Daniel and God in the lion's den. David and God against Goliath. The Old Testament is full of such experiences.

But the ugliest place of God's meeting was on Calvary. Crucifixion is not pretty. Fatigue, pain, humiliation, blood, sweat, and tears—all were there. But like Moses, how many thousands have seen that place of the skull as "holy ground"? Life's greatest detours—even death—is not able to outdo grace! It's there and it is no accident that out of some of the most tragic situations come the most profound experiences with God. Where did Jesus say, "Not my will but thine be done"? In Gethsemane! Where did Paul say, "I can do all things through Christ who strengthens me"? In prison! Now I don't know about you, but personally my deepest spurts of growth in faith have not come so much from my Galilees, where God clothed the lilies, "like Solomon in all his glory." But when the rains came and the floods descended and the winds blew and God was there, so my fragile house did not fall!

You hear all around these days of the sad state of affairs and that is by no means incorrect. But it's just so negative. Loss of confidence in our leaders, government, schools, the church—the world is falling apart. In such a world, we need to get a glimpse of the vision Jeremiah got of those souls who "found grace in the wilderness" because they knew about the law of resurrection, even before it happened!

I don't know why Moses' most revealing insight came, not from the royal life of easy street down in Pharaoh's house in Egypt, but out in the wilderness on a detour. But that's where he found grace. That's where he experienced the law of resurrection, and we can too.

A small boy once said, "Mommie, why are all the vitamins in spinach and not in ice cream where they ought to be?" The mother said, "I don't know, son. You'll have to ask God about that." But vitamins *are* in spinach and God is in every detour. Grace can be had in the wilderness. And you may want to remember that while you're on a detour.

---

[1]Wayne E. Oates, *Life's Detours* (Nashville: The Upper Room, 1974), p. 10. Used by permission.

5
Joshua: Something Better Speaks for Itself

Tevye, the main character in *Fiddler on the Roof,* played the part of a man who felt the importance of tradition, when he sensed it was time for a change. The scene where his daughters dared to be married without the services of the village matchmaker underlined in bold relief his need for ritual. Tevye experienced a dilemma. Torn between the heritage of his forefathers and a fatherly love for what he knew to be best for his daughters, he wavered back and forth, "Well, on the one hand, this," but "On the other hand, that," dialogue.

What Tevye experienced is a common occurrence for people on the move who face new and challenging situations. When Joshua told the Hebrew pilgrims "for you have not passed this way before" (Josh. 3:4), he characterized our day. We know what Joshua meant about passing by things his people never experienced before. We also know how Tevye felt. Being on the move makes it easy to identify with both.

Check it out in Joshua, chapters 1—3. Fresh from a forty-year stint of wilderness wandering, staring at those huge giants, the Israelites were about to enter the Promised Land, with all the glories and problems involved. Moses had died, and there they were poised at the edge of the Jordan to divide the land of their inheritance. Two things are noteworthy in chapter 3: change and ritual. First, the constant challenge of the new and different, "You have not passed this way before" (v. 4). And the second thing that made their faith vital in such a time, "When you see the ark of the covenant of the Lord your God being carried

. . ." (v. 3). Those two ingredients are important, especially to anybody in transition.

Let's talk about the ark. This great ancient shrine of the early Hebrew faith was portable because they moved so frequently, but it was highly cherished. They bowed down before that ark because they believed their God was in that box (Josh. 3:10-11). Some people still try to put God in a box or worship him from a television box. He's a lot more convenient that way. But in Joshua's day it was so appropriate. There can be no misreading of the lofty place the ark held in the Hebrew religion. It was so closely related to their faith in God that religion and the ark were virtually inseparable. Indeed in Numbers 10:35-36 the ark is directly addressed as "Lord." For awhile after they took Palestine, this attitude prevailed. King David continued Joshua's reverence for the ark by carrying it up to Mount Zion. Along the way a man dropped dead in his tracks because he dared to touch it. Likewise, King Solomon placed it in the heart of the Temple, the "holy of holies," as Israel's most priceless possession.

Then, as Israel moved away from the nomadic way of life toward a more centralized nation, things changed. So did her religion. Look to another day some six hundred years after Joshua and see the Hebrew religion developing. The prophets did not have the same reverence for the ark. The prophets faced the difficult task of reforming Israel's religion in keeping with her culture. For a sample of the prophets' feelings about Hebrew ritual read Amos 5:21-23, Micah 6:6-7, Isaiah 1:11,13-14, and Jeremiah 7:22.

Perhaps the most vigorous attack was by Jeremiah, who spoke of the ark this way: "When you have multiplied and increased in the land, in those days, says the Lord, they shall no more say, 'The ark of the covenant of the Lord.' It shall not come to mind, or be remembered, or missed; it shall not be made again" (Jer. 3:16). Jeremiah did not consider the ark vital to his faith, or anybody else's for that matter. What do you do with such a contrast? Both, obviously, were men of God. But they had two completely different reactions as to what makes religion real. Jeremiah wanted the ark forgotten because in his day God was not viewed as a localized deity. Rather, he was a universal God who needed no religious relic to aid in worship. Here we have a picture of the Hebrew religion being transformed into something better.

Joshua had his place. He represented the early days when religion was centered around a holy ark. The prophets had their place. They were also men of great religious faith who saw more clearly that God could be worshiped better without an ark.

How did this change in religion take place? Surely it wasn't without blood being spilled. Perhaps there was some "digging in the heels" along the way; a few closed minds; several doubters here and there—and maybe some even lost their faith completely. Such is the result of religious faith undergoing change.

But don't we always have these two stances in religion? The priestly ministry, characterized by Joshua. The prophetic ministry, characterized by Jeremiah. I think we do and I am claiming that it is a good thing that we have both, because we need both. I have an Accutron watch which has two hands on it. The large hand is faster than the smaller hand, but it takes both to tell "accurate" time. Likewise, we in the church would do well to strive for a balance between both temperaments.

First, let's consider Joshua, representative of the priestly ministry. Think of how he would feel if someone spoke of the sacred ark like Jeremiah did. Can you imagine what it would be like to go to Gilgal and tell Joshua as he lay prostrate before the ark that the day would come when people would serve God but would have no concern at all for the precious ark? Real faith without the ark? He wouldn't be able to see it. It's easy for you and me to look back in retrospect, but we do the same thing anytime we try to identify the Christian faith with our favorite brand of expression. And it is a great day when we recognize that true faith is greater than our pet arks.

It's a cause for celebration when we realize that living water can be carried around in different wineskins, separate from those to which we are accustomed. How would Baptists feel if someone said baptism by immersion alienates people who have been previously baptized by other methods? How would Catholics react to serving Mass to outsiders? It is always hard for one who depends on ritual to accept the criticism of a prophet who lives without the ark, yet not without faith. Joshua had faith plus an ark. Jeremiah had faith, but he needed no ark. Religion had changed and developed since Joshua's day. But the danger of majoring on ritual is that this spirit can become too rigid. We see it in the New Testament. Jesus came along in the prophetic tradition, refusing to pay homage to the arks of Judaism in his day. One example is sabbath observance, an ark that Israel's religion had hallowed through the ages. The rigid partisan reaction from Judaism was one of extreme defense of their "ark." They called Jesus a blasphemer, said he had a demon, and, in the name of "true" religion, crucified him! When the ritualist looks through such narrow blinders to the point that he can no longer see goodness in a different religious expression, then this is bad religion.

It is true that Jesus perfectly fulfilled the office of the High Priest. However, he did not do this through empty ritual or narrow partisanship. Jesus fulfilled the will of God by establishing a new covenant and calling all people, including the Jews, to enter the covenant. Jesus combined the best of the prophetic and priestly office. He gave us an example that we must not become too rigid or too critical. We must learn to love one another in the context of our relationship to God. More about this later.

For six years our church lawn mower took care of three yards. We really got our money's worth but inevitably the lawn mower gave up the ghost. Not being willing to cast it away, I ordered a new motor and when it arrived my first reaction was, "It doesn't *look* like the old lawn mower." I thought it was the wrong motor and was preparing to send it back. Then after taking a closer look I saw that Tecumseh Engine Manufacturers had made subtle improvements during the past six years. And while I, in fact, got a better motor, it still didn't *look* like the old motor. I made the mistake of not *being open enough to look for old truth in new covers.* A dependence upon ritual can cause that.

Sadly enough, we can accept this in lawn mower motors. But religion is another matter. Religion tends to make sacred everything it touches. "Only the motor that looks like my old one will do!" "If the King James Version was good enough for Paul and Silas, it's good enough for me!" Some people's religion often becomes narrow like that. It hallows its arks and often denies the contributions of archaeologists and biblical scholars who give us older and better manuscripts. Often contemporary versions of the Bible are not given their rightful place alongside the older versions. This resistance to the new and different is a powerful factor in modern religion.

Now I don't know what your ark is. But I know we all have them. It may be a particular theory of how we got the Bible; it may be a particular view of the second coming; it may be a particular version of the Bible; it may be a specific Baptist doctrine. Whatever it is, if it causes you to withdraw fellowship from and treat other Christians as less than brothers, it is a pet ark.

We need to make a separation at this point. It is necessary that we distinguish faith from one's ark. Keeping the faith is one thing, hallowing an ark is another. Jesus spoke once about wine and wineskins (Mark 2:22). His clear teaching was that new wine would demand new wineskins. It is interesting to consider some things that Jesus considered to be "old wineskins." Such pet arks were the sabbath, kosher food laws, fasting, and even the Temple (Mark 2:18-20,27-28; 7:1-6; 13:1-2). The sacred Jewish Temple would "pass away," but faith would remain. Things like faith, love, and commitment were considered to be "new wine" or what really mattered. Wineskins would have to be changed as they became rigid and useless. New wine called for new wineskins. "Old wineskins" are similar to the ark. Joshua should not be put down for his faith in his day. But we have outgrown the need for the ark of the covenant.

This is how I see Joshua in the scheme of things. One of the early explorers of this country was searching for the Pacific Ocean. What he discovered was a body of water not fifteen miles from where I live, the Chesapeake Bay. It was so broad that the explorer believed he had found the Pacific Ocean. Would anybody dare call him wrong? Think about it a minute before you do. In many ways he was right. There is a Pacific Ocean. But most importantly, he was moving in the right direction. It was 2,500 miles away, but he was headed right. That's the way I see Joshua—on the right track, but not there yet. He should be warned against rigidness, but not put down.

Now if the priestly spirit needs caution from becoming too rigid, the prophetic spirit needs cautioning about becoming too critical. Here's why. Transforming somebody's religion is no little thing. There is a real danger involved, namely, totally wiping out another's faith. Our forefathers called it "throwing out the baby with the washwater." Some prophets are in danger of doing that. The prophets caught a lot of flack because they castigated the old Hebrew rituals. Amos was told, "O seer, go, flee away to the land of Judah . . . and prophesy there; but never again prophesy at Bethel" (Amos 7:12-13). But we must realize something right here: *The only way to reform the practice of religion is with better religion.*

When Wilbur Wright went to France around the turn of the century, he demonstrated the superiority of his plane over the experimental models of the French. As it is when anyone introduces something new, he met with a good deal of hostility. But things changed after Wilbur showed what his plane could do. At first the crowd thought the Wright plane was going to crash, the way the wings dipped when he made sharp turns, but what was actually occurring was smooth banks and turns that the French had never seen before. As Wilbur Wright continued to gracefully circle the audience, the frightened gasps of the spectators turned to enthusiastic cheers. When he finally landed gently in a nearby field, the people crowded around his plane with great admiration. Even the proud French admitted the Wright brothers had come up with a better approach to flying and had a superior machine. The point is: something better speaks for itself. You don't have to push it. It will happen gradually as the light dawns. That's how folks grow in religion or anything else. Like Gamaliel said of early Christianity, "So in the present case I tell you, keep away from these men and let them alone; for if this plan or this undertaking is of men, it will fail; but if it is of God, you will not be able to overthrow them. You might even be found opposing God!" (Acts 5:38-39).

At the Air and Space Museum in the Smithsonian one can see that the Wright brothers' plane is now obsolete. Other developments came along that replaced it. That which was better spoke for itself. The same principle holds in religion. Nothing can reform the practice of religion except better religion. A deeper, more creative faith is the only thing that can transform religion. The ark of the covenant needed to be replaced by a faith that needed only a personal relationship with God. For this to happen, it takes time and a creative faith open to change, like that of the prophets.

There are two ways to wipe out somebody's ark. One way is to smash it to pieces with a condescending remark like, "That ark is nothing but sheer magic!" But the ark was more than that. It was a symbol of the best spiritual expression Joshua had to that day. He needed that ark to function. How could Joshua be expected to be any different? He had not been exposed to anything else. And if all the prophets can do is blast people's arks, it may only do away with their religion altogether. If the ark is to be laid aside, people who need the ark must be shown a better way. Those who would show the better way must do so in the attitude of Christ, not in a condescending or forcing way.

This is exactly what happened to me during my theological education, at Carson-Newman College and the Southern Baptist Theological Seminary. When I began my educational experience, I thought I knew it all. I had my mind made up; all I needed was the diploma. One of my professors called me "Elijah" because I wanted to call down fire upon his head! But when I hit the classroom, I began to react like Tevye. I realized my arks needed to be replaced, not smashed. My arks were not smashed, instead I was shown something better. Like the Wright brothers in France, my arks began to be replaced. I'll admit it took a lot longer for me to let go than some of the other "preacher boys," but I did let go once I became convinced of "something better." I will always pay tribute to the faculty at those schools for not smashing my arks, but helping me replace them with something better. This is an experience of life that I'll never forget.

Jeremiah wasted no time getting folks to update their theology. What Jeremiah did was to lift up a new concept of God that could not be mistaken as being localized in any kind of box. He showed us a universal God, a much more complete concept than Joshua was capable of formulating in his day. "Can a man hide himself in secret places so that I cannot see him? says the Lord. Do I not fill heaven and earth? says the Lord" (Jer. 23:24). The enlightenment of Jeremiah's day called for a more personal relationship with God himself.

Go back once more to Jericho and listen to the way Joshua prayed (Josh. 7—8). Like George Patton's heralded chaplain who prayed to God for assistance in killing his enemies, Joshua prayed like this because he was angry. He was angry because tiny Ai whipped the Hebrew army, and this wasn't supposed to happen. He wanted to know what went wrong. He wanted God to wipe out every man, woman, child, and animal and he would offer the entire city as a sacrifice to God. "Well, what kind of a person would pray like that?" you ask. But what did Isaiah do? He asked no such question. Rather he said, "He shall judge between the nations, and shall decide for many peoples; and they shall beat their swords into plowshares and their spears into pruning hooks; nation shall not lift up sword against nation, neither shall they learn war any more" (Isa. 2:4). That's how Isaiah said God really feels about war. He's against it! Nothing can reform religion but something better, and something better speaks for itself.

For too long it has been "us" versus "them" in our denominations. We are becoming more polarized and need to make up our minds to work together to make the coming years the "we" years. "We" need each other, and at bottom both the ritualist and the prophet want vital religion, the kind that produces strong Christian character and sends out servants to build up the kingdom of God. The kingdom is built by "we." It is torn down by "us." A genuine growing Christian is one who is able to pay little attention to folks' arks that divide us, but cares with all his heart about faith, which unites us.

The church, which has been likened to "the ark of salvation," may be more accurately characterized as a huge ocean liner trying to make its way up the river to port. It is too large to arrive on its own power so two little tugboats are needed to do the job. One on each side, tugging, pulling, to keep the ocean liner from running amuck in the shallows. The great ship of the church needs both the priest and the prophet. We need the prophet to stimulate us to use our imaginations and apply the gospel in more creative ways. If it is better, it will speak for itself. But the church also needs her traditions to remind us of the value of our roots. As creatures in transition, we too often mistake the Chesapeake Bay for the Pacific Ocean, but let us not forget that the Chesapeake was in the right direction. Thus, the need for both, to tug, criticize, and guide, in order to keep the right course. To do that is to have a church that is like the blue sky behind the passing clouds or the deep sea beneath the transient whitecaps. To do that is to develop a church with a faith that remains while our arks pass away. Both Joshua and the prophets have a message worth hearing. Have you heard it?

6
Ruth: An Outsider Becomes an Insider

Paul's experience portrayed in Acts 27 records a journey by sea and his arrival on an island in the face of danger and uncertainty. Acts 27 is transition at its best. Paul was making his way to get to a particular place but ended up on an island, forced to wait before proceeding further.

That Scripture passage is quite similar to the Communist takeover in Vietnam and the Vietnamese "Boat People," many of whom are stranded on islands. All of whom are in transition as refugees from their homeland to wherever they may go and be received. They hop from place to place and before long they are gone again.

I'll never forget the day I met a family sponsored by our church. The first telltale sign was the red button marked "CWS," for Church World Service, which paid their plane fare from Pendleton Marine Base in California. Here they came, carrying all their possessions in their hands, worn out, confused, scared, and excited all at once. Always meek. Always grateful. Such are the attitudes of those in the throes of transition.

Working with our refugees was an experience in itself. Neither Khoa nor Lan Van Le spoke English, but they could read it. So we wrote a lot of notes back and forth to each other. The first time I took them to the grocery store I went prepared to buy a lot of groceries, like fifty dollars worth. We came away with a few bags of rice and some carrots, totaling almost twelve dollars. In a matter of months Khoa was working, driving, speaking English and ready to move into his first apartment. We really didn't do that much with Khoa and Lan because they were paying their own way soon. Yet the culture shock they endured was stark and vivid. Although they are somewhat settled today, I'm sure they are still reeling from the anxiety of having been thrust from their home, hovering for a few months with no place to settle, totally dependent upon strangers for support, and just now beginning to become independent. Our role was to receive them something like Paul was accepted at Malta, "And the natives showed us unusual kindness, for they kindled a fire and welcomed us all, because it had begun to rain and was cold" (Acts 28:2). For someone whose journey had been long and weary that must have felt good.

I can think of no better parallel than Paul and the Vietnamese "Boat People" to help us understand the situation facing one of the most outstanding transients of the Old Testament: Ruth, the Moabitess, an outsider to the Hebrews. But her story is about a refugee outsider who became an accepted insider.

The transition begins when a Jewish couple named Naomi and Elimelech migrate to Moab to escape a famine in Bethlehem. Not long after arriving in Moab, tragedy struck. First they fled the famine, then disaster hit in the form of Elimelech's death. A few years later both their sons died, leaving three destitute widows. Naomi was grief stricken, as well as her two daughters-in-law Ruth and Orpah. Naomi has been considered by some interpreters as a feminine counterpart of Job, who passed from happiness to sorrow and whose faith was rewarded by more happiness again. The problem of the three women was made worse because in the ancient Middle East culture it was next to impossible for a woman to exist without a man's support and name. Thus, when Naomi heard the famine had ended in Judah, she decided to return home to live with her own people. Being an understanding mother-in-law, she urged Ruth and Orpah to stay in Moab where they had grown up. But widows fared no better in Moab. In a male-dominated society widows were treated as burdens to be borne, sometimes by the next of kin. By a stroke of fate, Mahlon's untimely death rendered Ruth almost helpless. Suddenly her value as a person was reduced and she realized, like the Vietnamese boat people, she had no place. She was not wanted in Moab or Israel. Alone, grieving the loss of her husband, facing a life of poverty at best and a burden to her kin at worst, Ruth became an outsider. Her marriage to a Jewish man made her an outsider in Moab. Because of her foreign birth she was an outsider in Israel and a second-class citizen. Since her marriage was mixed, she felt more ambiguity because her society pulled her in two different directions. Finally, unlike her sister Orpah, who chose to stay in Moab, Ruth decided the grass was greener in Palestine. In her search for security, neither place offered much hope. Still she was determined to go with Naomi and try to make a life in Bethlehem. Thus, Ruth learned to cooperate with the inevitable.

Now a question. Why would Ruth want to leave the place of her birth and go as an outsider with her mother-in-law to a foreign country and live with strangers? The rest of this chapter will be an effort to answer that question. Perhaps in the process you and I can gain some helpful insight about dealing with transition and how outsiders can become insiders.

One of the major themes of the book of Ruth is kindness and acceptance over duty and obligation. Naomi's kindness and acceptance of Ruth surely influenced her decision to become a transient. Ruth never forgot that she was a Moabitess, an outsider to the Israelite community, and I'm sure she wondered whether the Hebrews would accept her. Or more importantly, if the Hebrew's God would accept her, an outsider.

But Ruth was met with kindness which was typical of the familial kinship of the Jewish people. They have a long history of such kinship. The first two brothers in the Bible, Cain and Abel, illustrate it right off. Cain's popular question, "Am I my brother's keeper?" is answered, "You better believe it!" I saw this same sense of familial responsibility with the Vietnamese where it extended even to distant cousins. It was the same among the Jews—you *are* your brother's keeper!

Abraham and Lot exemplified this kinship on the day they parted, as Abraham said in deep respect, "Let there be no strife between you and me . . . for we are kinsmen" (Gen. 13:8).

Moses avenged the mistreatment of one of his own at the hands of an Egyptian guard. He put his own neck on the chopping block because of his kinship with his people.

The Old Testament is full of this kindness because of kinship and this is how they looked upon God. He too was kind, "As a father pities his children so the Lord pities those who fear him" (Ps. 103:13).

But a universal aspect creeps into this story, seen in Bethlehem's unqualified acceptance of Ruth in spite of her foreignness. Eight times in four chapters in the book of Ruth the point is made that Ruth was a foreigner. This could have been one influence on Jesus of Nazareth, who recognized that not just Jews, but all people are his kin. But the breakthrough in universal acceptance was first modeled in the book of Ruth. As a child I sang about it. "Red and yellow, black, or white. All are precious in his sight." As an apostle, Peter preached about it by opening the door to Gentiles in Acts 11. And Paul provides the highwater mark, "There is neither Jew nor Greek . . . slave nor free . . . male nor female; for you are all one in Christ Jesus" (Gal. 3:28). This is an acceptance that goes beyond the parochial, regional, national, and sexual barriers. Jesus built his entire ministry off the exact model of acceptance displayed in the book of Ruth years before. This acceptance was not confined to blood, color, or religion; it was universal, to all people.

Perhaps the main reason Ruth left home had something to do with Naomi's God. While Orpah wanted to go back to Moab with its many gods, Ruth was deeply impressed with the God of the Hebrew people. So she committed herself to that God. Telling Naomi of her decision, she said, "Your people shall be my people, and your God my God" (Ruth 1:16). That's another way an outsider can become an insider. Ruth committed herself to a God she never knew and even though she had no guarantee that she would even be accepted by him, she committed herself to God anyway. Just as Moses found grace in the wilderness (an unlikely place), Ruth found God in Moab and his commitment to her more than matched her commitment to him.

That's the way it is with God, you know. The more you commit yourself to God the more you find out what he's like and what he wants from you. God expects us to care for others like he cares for us. Which is exactly what Ruth did for Naomi. In caring for Naomi, Ruth discovered that the more she gave of herself, the more she received. On the cross Jesus saw his mother and John his friend. Both were lonely and isolated. In one of the most moving statements in the Bible, Jesus joined John and Mary to each other in an effort to dispel their loneliness. This is God's prescription for loneliness: outsiders become insiders by taking care of those in need. Being an outsider involves pain. But this pain is not deadened by drugs or denial or withdrawal —rather by taking responsibility for others in need along the way. Ruth and Naomi had each other and that's what happens when we get close to God—we get close to people. When we neglect a close relationship with God, we deny ourselves a resource of strength that could make a difference in life. One day a small boy tried to lift a heavy stone, but he couldn't budge it. His father, watching, finally said, "Are you sure you're using *all* your strength?" "Yes, I am!" the boy cried. "No, you're not," said the father. "You haven't asked me to help you." And those who don't commit themselves to God aren't using all their strength. But Ruth took advantage of this vital relationship and it helped her become an insider.

Another thing Ruth did that made her an insider was to join with God's community of faith. In our modern terminology we'd say she "joined a church." Joining a community of faith is certainly not easy for a stranger. Surely she was self-conscious being a Moabitess and a widow to boot. Her only strand of commonality was based on an in-law relationship to Naomi. She was poor and insignificant and had very little to contribute, but in spite of her apparent uselessness, she stubbornly insisted on joining with God's people. She said, "Your people shall be my people" (Ruth 1:16). So Ruth, the young widow who felt like an outsider, became an insider when she learned that belonging to God's community of faith is not based on national ties or racial background. This is how she dealt with her loneliness. She took the initiative to get involved with the people of God. Often the pain of loneliness cuts us off from God and other people because we focus on ourselves. This makes it difficult to communicate with others.

But the New Testament gives another picture where human suffering and isolation are countered by the fellowship of the Christian church. Church is where we are encouraged to share, not clam up like Sartre's residents of hell. The people who think they can get along without God's community of faith may well be on the road to hell. Those who make a god of self-sufficiency deprive themselves of the resources of faith in community with the people of God. The self-sufficient never pray. The self-sufficient never worship anything but whatever pleases them. The self-sufficient never give sacrificially except for what they can get out of it. That is hell.

Another thing the community of faith did for Ruth was provide a place for service. Ruth went to work immediately after arriving in Bethlehem, trying to eke out an existence for herself and Naomi by gleaning in the fields. Like Joseph in Egypt, her industriousness paid off, for she stood out among the gleaners to Boaz, who owned the field. Boaz became attracted to Ruth and extended her special favors.

But sharing in God's community of faith is more than gaining material possessions. Sharing involves openness between people so that trust and confidence can develop. Sharing calls for making room for one another in our hearts even though some are strangers. And sharing calls for the ability to receive as well as give, which is nonexistent in our "do-it-yourself" society.

Perhaps you've heard the tale of the man who died and went to both heaven and hell. In hell everyone had stiff elbows and were seated around a great banquet table set with all the trimmings. The same scene was true in heaven. In fact, you couldn't tell the difference in the places until the people started to eat. In hell there was total chaos as people tried in vain to get the food into their own mouths. But in heaven there was a tranquil peace and joy because each person fed the one sitting next to him. In hell they were selfish and independent. In heaven they were selfless and dependent. That's the difference and it can make all the difference between heaven and hell![1]

Ruth can only be characterized by those stiff-elbowed folks in heaven. Her character was grounded in her relationship to God (1:16), and to God's people, and to her loyalty to Naomi (2:11-12). She was willing to forsake her own country, her people, and her people's gods with no guarantee of anything in return. She had no idea that her poverty would be for a short time only, or that Boaz even existed. She had no idea that they would marry and deliver a son named, Obed, who would become the father of Jesse. How could she have known that Jesse would become the father of David, Israel's greatest king or that she would finally fall into the lineage of Jesus Christ, the Messiah of God's people. Which means David had Moabite blood flowing through his veins. The message of Ruth is: It's OK. There's nothing to get up-tight about, because blood didn't matter. Commitment, kindness, and acceptance did. And still does!

William Barclay tells a story about some soldiers who brought their friend to a Catholic cemetery in France to be buried during World War II. When the priest inquired into the deceased soldier's religion, he found that he was not a Catholic, thus, he could not be buried in that graveyard. The priest was sorry but firm. The soldiers then took their friend and buried him just outside the fence of the churchyard. The next day before leaving they came back by to pay their respects only to discover that they couldn't find the grave. While they were looking the priest came out and explained that he had moved the fence so that it would include the body of the soldier. By his actions he was saying, "He may not belong to my church, but he belongs to my God."[2]

That is the message of Ruth. It is a tiny book, containing only four chapters. But like perennial flowers it keeps cropping up with an eternal hardiness, showing that outsiders don't have to stay outside. There is a community where acceptance is available, built on the conviction of a God whose love overflows the limits that good people seek to impose upon him. This community represents a God who continually stretches the meaning of brotherhood and neighborliness until it includes all people. This community is the church, the new Israel, God's people who are a collection of transient outsiders in this day and age.

Allow me to illustrate today's church with an analogy. John's Gospel mentions that Jesus' robe was seamless. That means the maker had to weave each strand together without seams so that each thread had to fit in its own place. Such is the Christian church. God weaves all of us "Ruth-like" transients into a new community of trust and concern where we can share and serve through the Owner of that robe who now moves among us as risen Lord. He loves us into becoming insiders in a similar way that Boaz loved Ruth. He makes it possible for us to become part of his family, the church, just as Ruth was received into Bethlehem.

So Ruth's transition came to an end. We see it in Naomi's expression "The Lord grant that you may find a home . . ." (Ruth 1:9). Ah, home! This beautiful expression of home brings to mind a place of security and contentment—a settled place of permanence. The concept is adopted by the writer of Hebrews 4:9, who speaks of rest for the people of God. Naomi's use of the term meant a home, marriage, satisfaction in the companionship and love of a husband and healthy family. That was the end of transition for Ruth. As I look back on it, I can see why she left Moab. In retrospect we can say that she made the right decision. But she didn't know it at the time. All she had was her faith in Naomi's God and hope that she would be accepted. What Ruth did, anyone can do. We can be kind and accept the stranger, commit ourselves to God, and join in with his people. Hospitality is what it's called and it all depends upon whether we want to be on the inside looking out or on the outside looking in.

---

[1]Wayne E. Oates, *The Revelation of God in Human Suffering* (Philadelphia: The Westminster Press, 1959), p. 50.

[2]William Barclay, *The Letters to the Galatians and Ephesians,* The Daily Bible Study Series (Philadelphia: The Westminster Press, 1956), p. 135.

7
Absalom: The Curse of Impatience

Anytime you see a crowd of middle-age adults gathered you can bet that 50 percent of the time they'll be discussing teenagers! These turbulent days of adolescence are always good for a blast of criticism, for hopeless headshaking, all which makes most parents experts at playing "Ain't it awful?" I think this is happening because one of the most intense struggles with transition is occurring within today's youth. Negotiating the period from adolescence to adulthood has never been without its wrinkles, but something is going on today that makes the years of those from sixteen to twenty especially difficult, both on the parents who play "Ain't it awful," as well as the kids who make it seem awful. I am convinced that we are seeing a new thing. I speak existentially, as the father of two teenagers and the minister to families with teenagers. What we face today is unique, without parallel in the past.

A breach, not a gap, is the result. A vast cavern exists between many youth and their parents or anyone over thirty. These differences are not superficial. They go far deeper than the unusual dress, long hair, and wild music. We are experiencing a new approach to life. Things that middle-age people cherish and have been taught to respect in our society are taking a licking. Success, status, wealth, power, and security are being challenged today as worthy goals for life. That may not be bad, but what really bothers me is the spiritual breach. The rise in secularity has created a crisis of irreverence. I can think of no better symbol of this than the film, *Life of Brian,* a British production that is a witless attempt at sacrilege. It is crude but popular and that's what bothers me most. Hundreds of people, especially our youth are flocking to the movie and are enjoying the sarcasm toward anything religious, sacred, or traditionally cherishable—including Jesus Christ! The popular response to Monty Python's production is a prime example of the blasphemy and efforts to profane God that are taking place today. Reverence is taught no more. While this is primarily the fault of the older generation, still the youth are not without responsibility.

I can identify several characteristics of today's youth which separates them from the youth of thirty to forty years ago.

1. *The total emphasis upon "now" as opposed to an emphasis on the future.* Youth all over the world no longer assume as we did that the "good life" requires sacrifice. Why wait when we can have it now? Our credit-card culture has taught them they can have what they want when they want it. After all, if "now" is all there is, then self-control and willingness to prepare or sacrifice for the future are no longer valued. The traditional American way of life a few decades ago was future-oriented, which made sacrifice and hard work necessary. Long-range goals were common. But no more. The teacher's report card grade and the preacher's threat of hell fire no longer influence today's youth. And that may be good. But it is indicative of so many things happening at such an incredible rate of speed for our young people that they tend to think what they see is all there is.

What is missing is the normal progressive sequence to growing up that we older folks are used to. First, you go to school and get an education to prepare for the future. Then you go out and get a job and only after that are you supposed to marry. That's the way it *was*. Today, it seems like kids want to experience all of that at one time, rather than by natural progression. In their rebellion they fail to see that life cannot be lived without sacrifice. Sure Jesus sacrificed, but don't think that Judas didn't sacrifice. Esau, the progenitor of the "Now Generation," sacrificed his birthright for a "mess of pottage," which shows that this is nothing new.

Rebellion doesn't lead to freedom. It is merely another form of bondage. Most rebels tear down, protest, and destroy; this is only part of the way to freedom. It is freedom *from* but not freedom *for*. But this is one thing that has the adults shaking their heads in disbelief.

2. *"Do your own thing"* as opposed to *"Do your duty."* During his administration, Jimmy Carter invited student leaders of several universities and colleges across our country to come to Washington and discuss his proposal for registration in case of a draft. Next to the church, I cannot think of any institution that is seen by our youth as more authoritarian than the military. We have been without a draft for several years now, relying solely upon the voluntary services of our military. It seems that a potential crisis had developed because Russia hasn't exactly been resting upon her laurels. Consequently, a real danger existed because the voluntary draft hadn't worked. Zbigniew Brzezinski, Carter's military advisor was conducting an interview with the students and heard their protests, then closed the session by asking them this question: "If we had a voluntary registration, how many of you would sign up?" Only two raised their hands. "That," said the advisor, "is why we need the draft!"

How different that attitude is from the days before World War II when Uncle Sam pointed his finger saying, "I want you!" And he got them. America's youth in those days responded without protest and came readily because they grew up with "Do your duty!" rather than "Do your own thing!" It makes a difference. Today it's cool to be unpredictable, to be spontaneous, which are surely signs of distaste in a mass-produced society, and this may be good. But what it has led to is not good, namely, as some call it, "The Me Generation," which obviously refers to a whole generation of kids who are bounded on the north, south, east, and west by themselves! This, too, has the old folks wondering.

3. *The desire for instant intimacy as opposed to a "no touch" society.* While it took a long time for the older bunch to get from "I to Thou," today's youth do it instantly, or try to at least. Setting up tiny communes, playing house, establishing mini-marriages—boys and girls living together with all the privileges of marriage but with no commitments whatever. This is a testimony to their hunger for instant intimacy. But is intimacy something that can be obtained instantly? Some things can't be had right now! The high use of drugs, especially marijuana, is another example of false intimacy. With a fix, no courage is required to reach out to another person. It lessens the struggle to reveal oneself as it does in true intimacy. Samson wanted instant intimacy with Delilah, but ended up getting his hair cut off, a sign of his selfishness.

Here are some of the symptoms of an emerging way of life. Good or bad, they are here. It could be the thing of the future resulting in a new type of person, one I'm afraid who thinks he has outgrown God. And while we may not agree with the way they're going about it, we should take seriously the desire for freedom being expressed by our young.

Those familiar with the biblical message will recognize that this is not without precedent. The Bible too has its share of rebels. We have a good example in Absalom, King David's third oldest son. Perhaps from his life we can learn a way to prevent parents from saying "tsk-tsk" so much and begin to adopt Paul's attitude toward Timothy: "Let no one despise your youth, but set the believers an example in speech and conduct, in love, in faith, in purity" (1 Tim. 4:12). In surveying Absalom's freewheeling life, maybe we can gain some insight that might make it easier to negotiate this most difficult transition period from adolescence to adulthood.

How Not to Do It

Like Cain, Absalom is not a pattern worthy of imitating, but perhaps we can learn from his mistakes. We pick up the story in 2 Samuel 15—18, during the latter stages of King David's reign. In time, Absalom was the logical heir to replace his father and the Bible indicates he was well suited to do so. "In all Israel there was no one to be praised for his beauty as Absalom" (2 Sam. 14:25). The boy had quite a head of hair, like Samson, which was symbolic in more ways than one (v. 26 says he cut approximately four pounds a year)! But in reading about his life, I can detect a fatal flaw which led this young man who had so much going for him, who ". . . stole the hearts of the men of Israel" (15:6), to end up dangling by his hair from a tree! I guess this is what caused David so much grief, to see his son with so much promise end up blowing his only opportunity. Let's look at it.

First, Absalom, like Esau and Samson, was a card-carrying member of the "Me Generation." He grew up thinking *what I want is all that matters.* There were no boundaries on his desires. He had persuaded himself that whatever he wanted was right and whatever anyone else wanted was wrong. Although he was personally attractive (a "hunk" as today's kids call it), and was definitely gifted, Absalom's ego problem was what eventually brought him low.

This is a problem a lot of our youth experience because our competitive society, majoring on permissiveness and secularity has pointed them toward practical atheism. Absalom's father was called "a man after God's own heart," but obviously he placed too few restraints on his children. He was too busy running the affairs of the kingdom to raise his kids in the "nurture and admonition of the Lord." As a ruler David was brilliant, but as a father he was a tragic failure, which is evidenced by the tenuous relationship between him and his rebel son. But David's biggest fault as a parent has to be his failure to pass down to his children his sense of faith in God, a task Jesse felt strongly about. Consequently, Absalom couldn't get himself off his hands. He was attractive externally, but inside he was hollow.

This is certainly one response by youth in transition from the age of sixteen to twenty—a resistance to growing up. An infant is expected to be egocentric; self-centeredness is a necessary part of childhood. But if we are to become whole persons and not end up hanging from a tree like Absalom, we will grow out of this egocentricity. We will develop objective interests; learn to care for someone else besides "me"; discover some cause and values for which we may live or even die, if need be; to habitually forget our selfish desire in creative work that makes this world a better place for everyone, not just a better place for ourselves in this world. In her syndicated column, "Dear Abby" writes about this in response to a mother of three teenage boys in Cleveland who had committed eleven burglaries because "they had nothing to do." She responds:

Always we hear the plaintive cry of the teenager: "What can we do? Where can we go?" The answer is clear: Go home! Hang the storm windows, paint the woodwork, rake the leaves, wash the car, mow the lawn, learn to cook, scrub the floors, repair the sink, build a boat, get a job. Help the minister, Red Cross, the Salvation Army. Visit the sick, assist the poor, study your lessons, and when you're through, and not too tired, read a book. Your parents do not owe you entertainment. Your community does not owe you recreational facilities. The world does not owe you a living. You owe the world something. You owe the world your time and your energy and your talents so that no one will be at war, in poverty, or sick, or lonely again. In plain, simple words: grow up! Quit being a crybaby. Get out of your dream world and develop a backbone, not a wishbone. Start acting like a man or woman. You're supposed to be mature enough to accept some of the responsibility your parents have carried for years. They have nursed, protected, helped, appealed, begged, excused, tolerated, and denied themselves needed comfort so that you could have every benefit. You have no right to expect them to bow to your every whim and fancy. In heaven's name, grow up and go home!"

Abby obviously comes from the over-thirty bunch! But One a little older than Abby said the same thing with different words, "For whoever would save his life will lose it, and whoever loses his life for my sake will find it" (Matt. 16:25). The question during the difficult transition from adolescence to adulthood then becomes, How do I get from infantile self-centeredness to the maturity of a real person?

Like Absalom, more and more people never do. Even those over thirty still live out these selfish patterns, the "me-first" attitude. But it is a great day when a person gets himself off his hands. For years we live life as if surrounded by mirrors. Every way we turn we see only ourselves. What *we* feel, what *we* want, how *we* hurt. But the purpose of the years between sixteen and twenty is to change some of those mirrors to windows. Sadly, Absalom didn't have much help at this point. Consequently, he couldn't get himself off his hands. He remained a prisoner and never passed from a "mirror mind" to the "window outlook."

The "me decade" is producing all kinds of youth like Absalom who have no consciousness of God. Thus, they are obedient to their own impulses. "Whatever pleases me determines what I will do." "If it feels good, then I'll do it," so goes the slogan. The entire world of many youth today is like Absalom's thick head of hair—rooted in their heads. Both the world and their hair exist for their glory; both can be used for self-advantage. Their hair as a symbol of arrogance is seen in the ornate tomb Absalom had built for himself in an obvious effort to perpetuate his memory forever (18:18).

The next thing the Israelites were hearing were the words: "Absalom is king!" "Long live the king!" (16:16). He then mustered forces and ran his father out of Jerusalem, strutting through the streets, accepting the cheer of his subjects and moved to take over the royal palace formerly of his father. What is the first thing he does? I think it's significant. It is characteristic of the "me generation." Did he set about needed reforms in an effort to make Israel a better place to live? None of this. Absalom did what felt good, he raided his father's harem! This would be the grossest insult to David. Absalom revealed his playboy philosophy (2 Sam. 16:22). Instead of strengthening his hold and pressing out after David to ensure his defeat, Absalom raided David's harem. That was a mistake. For it allowed David time to regroup with his righthand warrior, Joab. While egocentric Absalom was satisfying his appetites with his father's harem, David was rallying his forces. He had only one request from his men, sensing that his fighters would vanquish the inexperienced forces of young Absalom, he pleaded: "Deal gently for my sake with the young man Absalom" (18:5). Sure enough, Joab's veteran soldiers routed Absalom's makeshift army. Before it was too late Absalom realized that it was "every man for himself," and characteristically he began to look out for old number one. He took off on his mule into the woods in an effort to escape (v. 9). He misjudged the low-lying limbs and jammed his hair into the branches, dangling helplessly in the breeze as his mule went on. Soon David's men were upon him and hesitated, remembering the request of the king. But Joab rode up with cold detachment and methodically thrust three darts into Absalom's heart.

The writer seems to say how odd that Absalom's main symbol of vanity, his hair, was the very thing that got him trapped. Further irony comes in the Absalom tragedy when the writer inscribes an eternal truth—the symbols of our pride will lead to our downfall. This is still true today. Parents stand by the wayside, like David, as their youth fall, like Absalom, by the wayside.

So Absalom was the youth who simultaneously didn't want to grow up, yet couldn't wait to grow up. He was a baby too long and tried to be a man too soon. But such is the struggle "modern-day Absalom's" face, espousing the same attitude: *"Now* is all there is. Grab all the gusto you can get. Why wait?" Absalom stands as a reminder of what impatience can do in a world where there is no justice. His lust for love, power, and security caused him to push things before their time. And we need to realize that you don't necessarily get there faster just because you push. What a lesson for us all!

Perhaps the final stab of sadness in the Absalom tragedy is

his burial. You remember how he had made previous plans for an expensive tomb for himself, so he'd be forever emblazoned upon the minds of his people? What actually happened, however, was not according to his conceited plans. Instead, his corpse was dumped callously into a pit. As one final gesture of disgust, David's men filed by one by one and threw rocks on his body until the stones completely covered him (v. 17). Absalom never made it to his magnificent mausoleum. There was no Marine band marching in cadence, behind a black, horse-drawn hearse. There was no one to mourn his death. Such is how some young people struggle into nothingness. It's enough to make the older generation shake their heads in frustration. David was frustrated because Absalom died the way he'd lived—alone. Living entirely to suit himself, that's what he got at death—himself.

There was one who mourned Absalom's death. David, his father. Probably more from guilt than grief, he cried, "O my son Absalom, my son, my son Absalom! Would I had died instead of you, O Absalom, my son, my son!" (v. 33). My guess is that bitter memories caused that cry of anguish. A pathetic cry of a bewildered parent who lost his son a long time before he caught himself between limbs in a tree. Wasted opportunities caused that cry. Back there when cute little Absalom could have been molded and encouraged to know God and care for others, his father was too busy to care himself. Father and son drifted apart because both were into their own egos. The breach never closed between David and Absalom because it ended in the death of the boy. David lived on, but the scar never healed.

Every parent needs to recognize how easy it is to lose a child. And every youth needs to see that there are thousands of ways to demoralize parents. We see it every day as families are disintegrating all around us. Where can we go for help?

How to Do It

The church has a word. As Christians we have a place to turn because of our model for authentic human life in the person of

Jesus of Nazareth. Born in a manger, died on a cross, no wealth or prestige to count, only those intangibles of strong character that today's society belittles. Yet, where his Spirit is, there will be a solution. His gospel is good news for every fumbling, rebellious child and every busy, uncaring parent of every generation, including ours. There is no better model for today's youth than our Lord, who also had to negotiate the same critical period of transition, sometimes called "the valley of the shadow of adolescence."

Luke tells us that Jesus did so by maturing in four different ways (2:52). Jesus increased physically, but also grew spiritually, mentally, and socially. This balanced approach to life enabled him to cope with the same kind of complexity we face in our day. Like the three blind men who were asked to give their impression of what an elephant felt like. The first man grabbed hold of the elephant's tail and said, "An elephant is like a rope." The second one picked up his trunk and said, "An elephant is like a snake." The third approached the elephant from the side saying, "An elephant is like a huge wall." The point is all of them were right in a sense, but if each one were absolutized, they would all be wrong.

It's always a mistake to oversimplify. We see it in Absalom's tragedy. Joab, David's general, had no patience with complexity. He couldn't understand how an enemy could be anything but the enemy. No more. No less. Enemies are to be killed before they kill you. That's the same adolescent attitude David had about Goliath the giant. But David had grown up into a complex world where issues weren't so clearly defined. Now the enemy was a son, his own flesh and blood. Joab brusquely swept aside such complexity by executing Absalom—the enemy. And when word reached David, he was crushed. A son, whom David cherished, was destroyed by Joab's simplistic approach to life. This is always the case when we narrow our outlook so that we deal with one thing rather than several aspects of things. In our complex society, often our "enemies" are also cherished. Things are linked together in many ways and the "Joab approach" will always make our "Davids" cry, because the Joabs rarely care enough to see outside themselves. So they are able to destroy in cold blood what another wants to redeem.

Further, Luke tells us that Jesus was the "friend of sinners" (15:2) and this caused problems with the religionists of his day, who separated sinners from God. How could a man be close to sinners and love God too? Just as Joab couldn't understand how David could love an "enemy," the religious leaders ended up doing the same thing Joab did to Absalom—Jesus was executed.

The balanced approach to life and death exemplified by Jesus of Nazareth was the best thing going for his day and ours. The only way Absalom grew was physically. He approached life by one dimension. We too will grow physically, automatically. Society sees to it that we grow mentally with our elaborate school systems. And socially, well we'll work overtime at that— anything to be accepted. But the church and the home must see to it that we grow spiritually. This can do wonders for getting ourselves off our hands. To trust God, to worship him in reverence, to give ourselves to something higher than ourselves is to change our mirror minds to windows. It is to make us outgoing instead of introverted. To feel a sense of connectedness with God is an experience that is at once humbling and exalting!

Today, parents still repeat the same mistake David made, failing to take responsibility to teach their children about God. Instead, parents make a mockery of the church and despise its people. I know the church is imperfect, it shames the ego a little, but it adds dignity to our personalities and helps make us whole persons. Balanced growth, patterned after Jesus, leads to the opposite of Absalom's egocentricity. I have never experienced anything that has done more to produce real people, whole people, balanced people with a sense of self-sacrifice as well as self-respect, as those who pattern their lives after Jesus. I will always be indebted to my parents for seeing to it that church was a part of my life.

The most promising model we need in our society today is that of a physician. A physician is one who relates paradoxically to patients. A doctor opposes disease, but at the same time values the health of the patient. A doctor's job is to destroy sickness and preserve the person. A doctor is both a preserver and destroyer at once. Such was David's approach to his "enemy" son. Like a doctor, he was involved with the dirty business of exposing himself to illness so that healing would come. But its too bad that Joab got to Absalom first. Such is the risk of life.

This, it seems to me, is the best way to "become a man," that Paul spoke about in 1 Corinthians 13:11. "When I became a man, I gave up childish ways." The thing to give up is the simplicity of extremes symbolized by Joab, and neither embrace society's values completely nor totally reject them in bitterness. We are to find our existence by living in the tension of the polarities of life. Paradox and complexity is the way we experience life in this world . . . living in the tension of opposites is where we find meaning. The sooner our youth learn that and pattern their lives after Jesus, the Great Physician, the better.

In an article by Abigail Trafford entitled "If Doctors Had Chosen Our Past Presidents," she reviews the book, *Presidential Courage.*[1] It is about the ailing achievers who held our nation's highest office. Men like Thomas Jefferson, James Madison, Chester Arthur, Andrew Jackson, Abraham Lincoln, Woodrow Wilson, and Franklin D. Roosevelt served this country in spite of illnesses ranging from epilepsy to cancer. Perhaps one of our greatest presidents, Lincoln, suffered from Marfan's Syndrome which would have probably killed him had John Wilkes Booth not done so sooner. The book shows how our history has been shaped by presidents who have been sick, lame, blind, and even close to madness. But they selflessly served and served well. That's quite a contrast to Absalom, the youth who was only interested in himself.

O God, friend of youth, give our young people a great vision, true insight into life's meaning and value; and help us who have been there before, to be their encouragers, good examples, and friends on the way, in the name of the young Prince of Glory, Jesus our Lord, Amen.

---

[1]"If Doctors Had Chosen Our Past Presidents," Abigail Trafford, *U.S. News & World Report,* March 3, 1980, pp. 45-48.

8
Jeremiah: Bloom Where You Are Transplanted

"Bloom Where You Are Transplanted" is a sign I saw on somebody's wall recently. It is an appropriate sign because ours is becoming a society of transplants. From grass and trees in the ground, and hairs on the head, to even the human heart, we are relishing the recent art of taking that which has good roots and renewing that which is worn out. My first experience with transplants occurred during clinical training experience in the Louisville General Hospital where I was assigned to the Renal Unit as Chaplain. It was a fascinating place to serve which afforded a laboratory of learning about people with a full range of perplexities . . . all yearning for a transplanted kidney. They called themselves "yendiks," which is the word *kidney* spelled backwards.

Getting a kidney was so important because it meant they would no longer have to come for dialysis treatments for six hours every other day in order to continue to exist. The dialysis process kept them alive but it also brought on a lot of suffering financially, mentally, physically, and spiritually. It could turn a tough Marine drill sergeant into a bitter vegetable. I'll never forget the time I saw my first real live kidney. It was on a temporary machine revolving back and forth so blood could filter through and keep it alive. The kidney had been taken from a twenty-one-year-old motorcyclist who was decapitated by a transfer truck and flown in from New York. In a matter of hours the kidney was transplanted into the body of a twenty-two-year-old woman who had previously undergone two transplant efforts. This one took and Mary Johnson is functioning well today, apart from dialysis. I was privileged to be her minister during the transition.

Similarly, I have had great success at transplanting trees in my yard. Finding small trees no bigger than a foot high, I carefully dig up the roots and place them in strategic areas of the yard. My favorite trees are dogwood, white pine, and hemlock. I have had a great interest in dealing with transplants.

But ours is a transplant culture. In the field of medicine and horticulture, we are finding that it is indeed possible to be uprooted from familiar surroundings and take root on foreign soil. The critical period for trees is just after the roots are planted. I try to supply a lot of water during the first few days to ensure rootage. With organ transplants the first few days become critical as the body tries to reject it. The kidney has a fantastic sense of "not me" and certain drugs can be administered to counteract that. But the issue is the same with both trees and organs—to make the roots take hold on foreign property. This critical period begins when the roots are torn up and placed down in another place. It is not complete until the roots take hold where they are transplanted. There is always the danger of rejection.

Blooming where you are transplanted was the situation which faced the prophet Jeremiah, who lived in a time of religious transition and tried to reform Israel's religion with better religion. I think he did. Perhaps it would be helpful to consider more concretely Jeremiah's prescription for being transplanted.

Jeremiah's instructions got him into a heap of trouble. His first experience in ministry at Anathoth had disastrous consequences for him because his message was not a popular one with the Jews. But because he was faithful in preaching it, he became an expert on uprootedness.

We can benefit from what he learned because Jeremiah put his thoughts down on paper. He wrote a letter and sent it over to Babylon for the Hebrew exiles to read: "These are the words of the letter which Jeremiah the prophet sent from Jerusalem to the elders of the exiles, and to the priests, the prophets, and all the people, whom Nebuchadnezzar had taken into exile from Jerusalem to Babylon" (29:1). A word from the Lord to hundreds of Jewish exiles, huddled together, with scorched memories of their deportation, the noise of pagan idol worship constantly in their ears, and their spirits crushed by the power of Babylonian military warfare. Jerusalem had fallen. Solomon's Temple was gone. The holy ark, priesthood, and sacrificial cult no longer existed.

The captors taunted: "Sing us one of the songs of Zion" (Ps. 137:1-4). The Jews were ruthlessly torn from their native Palestine and taken to Babylon as prisoners of war. Their humiliating defeat was rubbed raw by the separation from their homes and Zion's holy Temple. Had they not always gone there to see God—in the holy of holies? Now, uprooted from God's dwelling place, they were homesick believers. "Sing you a song? How can we sing the Lord's song in a strange land?" That is the challenge of learning to put down roots. How could they go on? How could they continue to hope?

Well, Jeremiah wrote to tell them how. Listen to a letter God revealed to Jeremiah to read to people in need of roots. "Thus says the Lord of hosts, the God of Israel, to all the exiles whom I have sent into exile from Jerusalem to Babylon" (Jer. 29:4). He told them to do three things:

1. "Build houses and live in them; plant gardens and eat their produce" (v. 5). The first thing we must do when uprooted is—the very next thing that needs to be done. Do what is necessary. Plunge in. Don't wait for the future. Get started. Make the most of things right now. Waiting is the enemy of transition. In a sense, former football coach, George Allen was right: "The future is now," which is another way of saying, do the best you can with what you have. The little everyday jobs, like planting gardens and eating the crops are important. Sometimes the only thing we can do is work. But if we do it, Jeremiah says there is healing in it.

2. Next, verse 6 says, "Take wives and have sons and daugh-

ters; take wives for your sons, and give your daughters in marriage, that they may bear sons and daughters; multiply there,
and do not decrease." In transition there is nothing as important
as fellowship. We can rely on our family and our church family.
God advises it for folks struggling with transition. "See to your
wives and daughters and sons." No time, meantime or other-
wise, must be allowed to sever, damage, or strain our relationships to our wives and children. The transition of grief must not
soak the family with bitter tears. Anxiety at being unable to
move or find meaning in your work must not bring emptiness
into the family relationship. Beware of imposing your pain
from meantime wounds on your tender ones. There is a future
to be prepared for—even in Babylon. We forget the future
while we're living without roots because we leave before the
show is over. Yogi Berra said, "It ain't over till its over." Judas
quit on Jesus before Jesus said, "It is finished!" And we still
suffer this same malady today—we lack the power to see things
through. We give up before God is done. But we always have
a future, no matter how bleak. It's there—God told Jeremiah to
live like it. Prepare for the future.

3. Now for the shock treatment. Here is the heresy of God's
wisdom, "But seek the welfare of the city where I have sent you
into exile, and pray to the Lord on its behalf, for in its welfare
you will find your welfare" (v. 7). Can you believe it? What a
word for homesick Jews! Some comfort for those hungering for
the ark and the Temple in Jerusalem. This is rank heresy to
such! It is treason! He was accused of "treason" more than once.
So was Jesus. Can you imagine "seeking the welfare of a city"
which uprooted you from your homeland and everything that
is sacred? No matter how you look at it, this is hard to take.
Here are these exiles, loving Jerusalem, hating Babylon, and
then God has the gall to ask them to pray for the very people
who took them captive? Sounds a lot like another, who advised
his followers to pray for their enemies. That man was certainly
familiar with God's letter to Jeremiah . . . for he knew the
wisdom of praying for one's enemies, instead of cursing them.

I would interpret verse 7 to mean that God intends for us to put down roots where we find ourselves. I was visiting with a new neighbor recently and the man said, "I've lived all over the United States, being in the military, but my home is right here on Post Lane, at the moment." Now that's what verse 7 is getting at . . . and its interesting, that the new neighbor took his family to seek out a church the first Sunday they were here! That says something, too, doesn't it? But God pity the poor folks who drift through life . . . how many other newcomers have you heard say: "We are just passing through; we have no time to put down roots; we'll only be here for a year or so, no sense getting established if we're just going to be uprooted again." Well, let me tell you something. To do that is to fly in the face of the clear instruction of Almighty God! There will be no escape from the hell of not putting down roots where you are. As long as the Jews sing, "How can we sing the Lord's song in a strange land?" they will have problems. Now your roots don't belong where they used to be or where you're going to be. Roots belong where you are. You've got to grow where you're planted or transplanted. And Jeremiah said that if you can't do that, then there's no hope for you in Babylon or anyplace else. Transition has whipped you! If the Jews can't pray for Nebuchadnezzar they may as well forget their religion of a universal God.

In the movie, *Escape From Alcatraz,* Clint Eastwood portrayed a man who put down roots where he was, although it happened to be in prison. The result was an escape from Alcatraz, the only man to ever do it successfully. He did it by putting down roots in the interim. This third word from Jeremiah's letter is the key to meantime living. Without it there is no hope.

Why do we resist putting down roots where we are? We simply can't betray our former estate. Some hate their jobs, so they don't put down roots. Others can't stand where they live, so they don't make any friends. Still others resist intimate involvement, so they don't participate in church fellowship. People who have no present roots betray their colors quickly, for they are vagabonds like Cain, living "East of Eden"; they haven't learned to live in transition, and they are half alive.

But it must have been tough on those Jews in Babylonian captivity. Verse 7 is hard stuff to swallow for folks whose culture changes faster than people can move from one apartment to the next. But Jeremiah says there is healing in it. There's healing in all of it. He gives us three tangible things we can do in time of transition:

1. Do what you can—what needs to be done—"Build houses . . . plant gardens" (v. 5).

2. Rely on the fellowship, and plan for the future—"Take wives . . . and . . . multiply" (v. 6).

3. Put down deep roots right where you are—"Seek the welfare of the city where I have sent you into exile . . ." (v. 7).

Burch Cooper, a seasoned minister who sat in on my ordination, gave me some timely advice: "Son, do everything like you were going to be there forever." Jeremiah said that is the way to healing. Pray for the welfare of your Babylon—for if it prospers, you will too!

There's one other word worth noting in Jeremiah's letter: "For thus says the Lord: When seventy years are completed for Babylon, I will visit you, and I will fulfil to you my promise and bring you back to this place. For I know the plans for you, says the Lord, plans for welfare and not for evil, to give you a future and a hope" (vv. 10-11). Life has its fill of uprootedness. Transition will come to an end. It will come to an end when God comes to Babylon.

God says the captivity is to be endured, conquered, and redeemed. To look around and see what needs to be done and do it, put down some roots, and seek the peace of the city as our own peace. For there will be an end to the "waiting." The seventy years will pass and when they do, God said, "I will come to see you." God himself will come to participate in our captivity—as a man, speaking the word of men. Here's the lesson: God already came 2,000 years ago and God is even now at work in all our captivities—he's right here in our Babylon to help us learn to live in transition. "Then you will call upon me and come and pray to me, and I will hear you. You will seek me and find me; when you seek me with all your heart" (vv. 12-13).

Let's consider again that piercing question: "Can we sing the Lord's song in a strange land?" We can if we discover that "they who wait on the Lord shall renew their strength" (Isa. 40:31). If we learn that he is a universal God, not confined to any place; that he is closer than our very breath; that "where two or more are gathered," he is in the midst of them; that they can pray to him and be heard by him—this faith becomes the foundation for life that can be lived in any Babylon. When we discover that God is universal, ever present, and the redeemer of all mankind and not just a private possession of our own clan which we keep in a convenient little box.

When we leap over the barriers of our provincialism which separates us from accepting and understanding people of different color, custom, and clan—we can sing the Lord's song!

When we let God lift us up like he did Peter into a vision of God that is "no respecter of persons," a God who has not made any man common or unclean—we can sing the Lord's song!

When we discover our kinship with our captors, like Paul did in the house at Caesarea—we can sing the Lord's song! Later on, that same man wanted to take the gospel to Spain. Instead, he found himself in a Roman prison. With locked doors surrounding him, he began a ministry of writing and in that period of unsought opportunities he took advantage of his imposed inactivity. It was during this time that he wrote much of the New Testament. Paul knew how to sing the Lord's song! This was the truth that hit the woman at the well who couldn't understand how Jesus, being a Jew, could speak to her, a Samaritan woman. The old wineskins of the Jewish faith were too small to hold the new wine—this view of God as Redeemer of all the people of the world. No one is excluded! When we realize that—we can sing the Lord's song!

We've got to quit depending upon our self-made security

systems that keep us from putting down roots. They can be blasted away from us at any time. We have no enduring city here. We must seek out a church family of God that transcends blood ties, a church home that reaches beyond our own city limits, and a city whose "builder and maker is God." We must learn to sink our roots into the greatness of God, even though we may be transplanted. We can still bring forth fruit in due season so that our leaves won't wither. When we do that, we can sing the Lord's song! Then as the writer of Revelation says: "The leaves of the tree were for the healing of the nations" (22:2).

9
Nehemiah: Character for Rebuilding Broken Walls

In his book *When the Road Bends,* Karl Olsson writes, "Transitional trauma is what happens to people who have trouble coping with change, and it's becoming more common in our time."[1] Then he lists several ways "transitional trauma" affects American families. Among them are those experiencing divorce, the business world, military and governmental workers, personnel whose job keeps them on the move, and *people whose vocational goals have not been reached, who have to lower their vocational expectations.* The trauma caused by transition in one's vocation is what I'd like to discuss in this chapter.

I remember how excited I was when the University of Tennessee hired John Majors as the new head football coach and the hope this move represented toward restoring Tennessee football to its normal place of prominence. To Tennesseeans, it was like "Bear" Bryant going back to Alabama. It was a case of "local boy makes good" and is returning to his alma mater. His list of accomplishments on the gridiron were many. He was a real hero during my high school days and a good model young people could follow. Majors led the Volunteers to an undefeated season, a berth in the Sugar Bowl in New Orleans, and a lofty ranking in the national polls. But Majors was even more successful as a coach. Everywhere he went, losing football programs were turned into winners. First at Iowa State; then at Pittsburgh, where in 1976 he led the Panthers to an undefeated season and number 1 ranking in the country. Not long after that he was elected "Coach of the Year." Majors could not be any more successful. He had achieved the heights in his profession and he was still a young man.

This is why the state of Tennessee went wild at the announcement with crowds breaking out in singing, "When Johnny comes marching home again, hurrah!" Tennessee's football program was definitely sagging under Coach Bill Battle and had been for four years; folks were tired of crying, "How long, O Lord?" Before Majors was signed, Battle had to be released from his contract, which thrust both coaches and their families as well as the athletic programs of two major colleges into transition. Although both coaches experienced transition, Battle's was a lot more traumatic than Majors'. Majors came as a success, bringing vitality back to a program in disarray. Battle left his vocation not nearly so successful as the UT alumni had intended. He left coaching altogether, moving back to his native Alabama going into business there. Bill Battle probably experienced great trauma because he was forced to abruptly change jobs. Majors' trauma was more subtle, but just as real. He faced a rebuilding job at Tennessee, but more importantly, he faced the expectations of the Tennessee people, many of whom expected instant success like Majors had at other colleges. Well, success was not instant. The team is still trying to turn the corner, trying to achieve consistency, but such is the trauma of rebuilding.

I went through all that to say this: Coach John Majors' experience in moving from Pittsburgh to Knoxville, Tennessee, is not unlike Nehemiah, one of the more attractive men of the Old Testament. A Jewish exile deported to Babylon around 470 BC. Nehemiah was familiar with "transitional trauma" connected to vocation. After the Persians came to power, a spirit of cooperation with the exiles afforded Nehemiah the opportunity to progress in a foreign country much like Joseph, his ancestor, did down in Egypt. Nehemiah became a ranking officer of influence with Cyrus the king. Upon hearing from a traveler of the sad state of affairs back in Israel, Nehemiah was so adversely affected that it was noticeable from his appearance. The king saw it and mentioned it to Nehemiah, who took advantage of the king's concern by requesting permission to return to Jerusalem for the purpose of rebuilding the walls to the city. In those days walls were absolutely necessary for survival. The only other option was to build near a river or up on a crest of a hill which afforded natural barriers to the enemy. An ancient city without walls was vulnerable to anyone who wished to plunder. Cyrus, knowing this, granted Nehemiah permission as well as a safe passage including a document that provided for the materials to carry out the construction project.

So Nehemiah went to rebuild something that was vital to his people, and this was the beginning of his struggle with "transitional trauma" in his vocation. He was stepping down from a role of leadership in a foreign country where he was cupbearer to the king to become a contractor with a rebuilding program to help his people. He left an established life in Babylon and went to Jerusalem where things were every bit as bad as he had heard. Enemies were gobbling up the spoils of a hapless city without walls, the people were discouraged, and there was very little hope of improving the situation because they were so poor.

Here we have a classic example of something we transients are too familiar with: overwhelming demand in the face of too little resources. But the people of God faced this situation before and after Nehemiah and they will face it again. Moses faced it in the wilderness with a huge throng of freshly liberated slaves on his hands and no way to feed them. Back then there were no McDonald's to quench the "Big Mac attacks," but God provided his own solution in the form of manna. Later on, God's Son faced a similar situation near the Sea of Galilee where he fed 5,000 people with a young boy's sack lunch that consisted of five barley loaves and two fish. But God provided in the wilderness and he provided for the 5,000 on the Galilean seashore and he will provide to those who respond to him in faith today. Manna was God's nurturing a vulnerable people who had learned to live on the edge of survival. Nehemiah lived on that edge. He had a job to do. His task was to construct new walls. Not only did he face a major construction project, but also he had to do it with people whose spirits were defeated in the presence of enemies.

But Nehemiah pulled it off because he had learned to improvise, thus, he stayed with it until somehow he got the job done. He didn't do it by doing anything unusual or great. He did it by being faithful to little things, things that anyone can do. If we can't do great things, we can do small things in a great way. So Nehemiah organized the people and gave them a new hope with his strong character. He put them to work; half of them worked while the other half stood guard. When progress became apparent, the enemy tried blackmail by insisting that Nehemiah come down off his wall to consult with them or else they would send back word to Cyrus that he was subversive. In response, Nehemiah said, "I am doing a great work and I cannot come down" (Neh. 6:3).

Now what we have here is a picture not only of Nehemiah's character, displayed by not coming down, but a frequent theme of the Bible. That theme occurs whenever somebody achieves something great or accomplishes something noteworthy and finds a counterforce seeking to pull him down and destroy his work. Nehemiah wasn't the first to be asked to come down off the walls of character. Adam and Eve met the same proposition in the beginning. They came down. It was the exact challenge hurled at Jesus when he was urged to come down from the cross. But he would not come down. Here is a nutshell of the basic moral struggle of every person and this seduction is still with us and is no different from the day Nehemiah heard it from Jerusalem's wall.

To Nehemiah's credit, he did not come down. He realized he had come too far and worked too hard and spent too much time to get those walls up to come down. Once he got on top, he guarded his priceless position with great care. It was a position more easily lost than won. Character isn't something that can be bought. It is not for sale. Character and ingenuity take time to develop and the quality of life that comes from a meaningful vocation is the same. Many plodding steps are required to get to a good position but it only takes one step to come down.

What can we learn from Nehemiah's transition as he struggled to change vocations and reconstruct broken walls? For one thing, Nehemiah's experience isn't just theoretical for many of us in transition. We have experienced it firsthand and understand well what he must have felt. The old saying, "There's plenty of room at the top" doesn't have much to do with reality. The fact is, getting to the top is hard to come by and the road to the top is crowded. The closer you get to the top the more folks will try to pull you down. Thus, out of necessity, many of us will have to be content with never making it to the top.

This causes problems. It makes it difficult to select a vocation because everyone wants to do something that has distinction. The trouble is that the options and variables are so numerous that many are baffled by them and the result is, people back into their vocations in a hit-or-miss fashion; relying more on luck than definite choice. I think we'd be surprised at the number of people who can say, "This is my work and I'm doing it because this is what I chose to do."

Another problem is some who made a conscious choice, discover in later years that they made the wrong choice. A frequent problem of counselors is to deal with those who feel trapped in a job they don't enjoy. Often, the solution is bleak. Hemmed in by time and economic factors, there is very little that can be done but tough it out until retirement—which might be a significant number of years. This makes each hour spent on the job resented because of the turmoil caused by drudgery and dread. So a lot of folks either made no choice at all or having made one made the wrong one. Consequently, millions ask: "What will I do with my life?" That question lies at the root of a lot of transition today, for people hop from job to job in search of meaning and I believe it needs an answer. I don't claim to have one, but the Bible does offer some help here in the form of personalities who have grappled with similar problems in their

life's work. Here are some things we would all do well to remember.

1. The fullest meaning in life doesn't come from being *exceptional* but from being *faithful* to what we do have to do. Not
everybody can be exceptional, but we can all be faithful. Nehemiah was faithful to his task. He did small things in a great
way—things we all can do. He worked hard, organized, and
improvised when things didn't go right. Because of this, he
found meaning in what he did.

Jesus told a helpful story that illustrates this same truth. It is
about a man who went on a journey and entrusted his property
to three workers. He gave one five talents, another two talents,
and yet another one talent. The five-talent man was faithful
and doubled his talents while the boss was away. So did the
two-talent man. But the one-talent man buried his talent in the
ground (Matt. 25:14-28).

We make much of the five- and one-talent men and are prone
to overlook old number 2, the middleman of the story, and
that's sad, because he's the one most like you and me—average.
But he was faithful with his two talents. He used his gift wisely
and was rewarded and fulfilled because Jesus' point is simply
this: You can derive as much meaning from using what you
have to the fullest as the person who has been given more.

We are influenced by our achievement-oriented society
which drives us to the top to be number 1. But Jesus teaches us
that you can find meaning by being faithful, not exceptional.
You don't have to be a star to be in God's show! Strong character that results in inner peace means more than all the prestige
in the world. Anyone can have it if one will do what that
two-talent, average man did with his gifts: all he could with
what he had.

2. Another thought from Nehemiah and the two-talent man
is: Our task in life is not to find meaning *within our work* but
to find meaning *within ourselves.* In other words, meaning in
our work doesn't come from the job itself, but from inside the
worker. That's not easy, but I believe it is possible most of the

time. If it's not possible, then we should certainly consider changing vocations. But circumstances are such that some people can't change. Their choice is to "bloom where they have been planted." Then they have to improvise.

I can think of no better example than a freak accident on the Metro Subway System in Washington, D.C. It happened this way. The operator stepped outside the train to check the track, which was a mistake, because when the computer saw a green light it promptly closed the door with the operator locked out of the train as it started to move. The train took off and stopped at the regular stations but let nobody off because the operator wasn't on board to open the doors. The runaway train was destined to keep running around and around unless someone intervened. It just so happened that a young woman named Kilena Loveless sized up the situation, ingeniously picked the lock to the engineer's cab with a barrette from her hair and stopped the train. There were no injuries because she was creative enough to improvise. Talk about the world in a grain of sand! In this episode of the supreme adequacy of a hair barrette, you have just about everything that's right and wrong with us and our times. No doubt a computer can run the subway. The only thing wrong is, a computer has no judgment. The good part comes with the woman who had a hair barrette, a brain, and initiative. She was alert. She kept her eyes open. She was ready for any emergency an unreliable universe may toss in her lap. She acted quickly and decisively to make do with whatever she had. What Kilena Loveless did with her hair barrette is what people need to do whose work has grown dissatisfactory.

Normally such work conditions would cause us to think that the grass is greener elsewhere—so we quit our job, opting for a change in geography. Then we change our identity and our circumstances, thinking life has to get better. Sometimes it does, but it won't if you carry your problem with you! And that's the problem. Most of the time a geographical change is not the solution, while an internal one is. Frequently, the problem is not in the job but in the worker, so when the person moves the problem is still there.

Last year the Prince George's County School System, the largest in the nation, closed several of the elementary schools in an effort to comply with legislation that called for fewer schools. This decision affected my family in a direct manner since my wife was head secretary of one of the schools which was closed. I was impressed by all the feelings and situations this kicked up in her. Abruptly, she was uprooted from a familiar place where she was well established; where her identity was clear; her work description was routine. She had earned respect from her peers and many of the teachers looked up to her almost like a "big sister." She had a great working relationship with the principal and everyone in the school because she's just a terrific secretary.

Suddenly all that was gone. An entire community was wiped out as the school was closed. This meant instant transition. For months she didn't know if or where she would work. Finally, when word did come that she had been placed in a school nearer our home, we felt pretty good about it, considering what it could have been. But from day one, things were not working out. For any number of complex reasons deeper than anyone can fathom, my wife was miserable. I counseled her to stick it out; give it a chance and see what develops, but to no avail. Then I changed my tune and advised her strongly to put in for a transfer, which she did. And lo and behold, after that happened she had a session with her principal to "clarify matters" a bit. Since placing her transfer she has had three job offers and turned them all down because Kettering was looking better and better! The work is still the same. The change occurred in her. Often it's that way, those who find life most meaningful are those who make it meaningful where they are. The apostle Paul rose to great heights while serving a prison sentence. Jesus did God's will while traipsing across the dusty hills of Galilee. Both knew how to improvise, which is the secret Kilena Loveless discovered. The key to life is not finding a meaningful place, but making the place meaningful where you are.

3. Another thing Nehemiah and the two-talent man did that we can do is to *commit ourselves to something bigger than we are.* Facing an insurmountable task, Nehemiah left a comfortable life in Babylon to cast his lot with the Israelites in Jerusalem. In Babylon he had a job. In Jerusalem he had a cause. And my hunch is that life took on new meaning for him when he changed. When you do something that contributes to a good life for others, that makes the world a better place for somebody else, that perspective makes what you do take on added meaning.

One reason many folks are dissatisfied around us is because they have nothing for which to live—outside themselves. Their life has no useful purpose. It's a heavy burden to bear unless you find something to give yourself to; something that you can see where you can make a contribution—no matter how small. If you can, life will become worthwhile. For life to be fulfilling, you have to feel that what you do makes a difference.

That was the theme of the film *Running,* starring Michael Douglas. He played the role of an insecure person who couldn't hold down a job. He quit everything he tried to do. He quit studying for a vocation in medicine because that's what his parents wanted him to do. He quit his marriage because his wife was tired of his quitting. Michael was tired of it too. Finally through running, he realized the reason he had no consistency. He was afraid to lose and was doing something that others wanted him to do. He ran because it was one thing *he* wanted to do. And he did it well; so well, in fact, that he was selected to represent our country in the Olympics. He was determined no matter what, to finish that race. Finishing the race symbolized so many things. As fate would have it, being in first place he fell, dislocating his shoulder. But Michael got up and crossed the finish line even though the official race was completed. He didn't have to be the best. He did it because it was important to him. That made the difference. As the movie ended, life became worthwhile.

So the answer to "What will I do with my life?" is simply this: something useful. The most pathetic people I know are not those like Nehemiah who are overworked, but those who have nothing useful to do.

The most blessed people around are those like Nehemiah who said later on: "Go your way, eat the fat and drink sweet wine and send portions to him for whom nothing is prepared; for this day is holy to our Lord; and do not be grieved, for the joy of the Lord is your strength" (Neh. 8:10). These are the ones who meet the challenge of "transitional trauma" by:

1. Being faithful rather than exceptional,

2. By finding meaning within themselves rather than in their work,

3. And by giving themselves to something beyond themselves.

Nehemiah had climbed to the top and would not come down. Perhaps that is why one of the frequent biblical images is the mountaintop. The Ten Commandments were cut in stone and given to Moses up on Mount Sinai. Jesus preached the Sermon on the Mount, and several times went up on the mountains in Galilee. The mountaintop is a sound image for it depicts what I've been talking about, namely character, courage, and lofty ideals. It takes awhile to climb a mountain, just as it took time for Nehemiah to rebuild his wall. But once he got up there, he would not come down!

---

[1]Karl A. Olsson, *When the Road Bends* (Minneapolis: Augsburg Publishing House, 1979), p. 32.

10
Mary: Learning to Stand Alone

We live in a mixed-up world. While we have many accomplishments and have made great advances, in other ways we are retreating. People look at our sprawling cities, airlines, the maze of freeways, and shopping centers and conclude that we've come a long way. Yet, there are people who live in a community for years and never get to know their neighbors. They go to work, drive around, eat out, watch television, see a movie, go to parties, and continue to say their lives are empty. From Maine to Florida, from the East Coast to the West, people are searching. They move from one town to another, from one neighborhood to the next, join clubs, pop a pill, go shopping in crowded stores, take a drink, but still the pain is there. Loneliness is there because loneliness is a real part of transition.

Wayne Oates said that we as human beings have the distinction of standing erect, which we learn to do right early.[1] We can stand up but we've not learned how to stand alone. Paul urged us to "take the whole armor of God, . . . and having done all, to stand" (Eph. 6:13). It is one thing to stand, and another thing to stand alone. We have not yet learned to fully enjoy life or build lasting relationships. Statistics reveal interpersonal relationships are worsening, evidenced by a rapidly increasing divorce rate. Even nations are finding that international relations are worsening.

Someone suggests that part of the problem is related to the time modern Americans spend in front of television sets. There we meet some crazy mixed-up values that tell us life is a magazine, gusto is a drink, power is a candy bar, and joy is a detergent, my sin is a perfume; and the real thing is a soft drink! Watching television is a spectator activity and too much time in front of the tube hinders human interaction which must constantly be developed and improved. Nowdays they even have church on television, so you can "go to church" without leaving your home. Merely observing folks worship on a screen is no substitute for getting to know each other, sharing with each other, even fussing and fighting with each other. Learning to love and relate successfully to people is what life is all about and this is hindered by an overabundance of time before television sets.

The high degree of mobility in our society, where one out of five families change residence each year, has reduced the traditional family and neighborhood friendships to zilch! Consequently, our mixed-up modern affluence, high mobility rate, and overexposure to television contributes to a new form of loneliness. People are bored and lonely while simultaneously being surrounded by others. Never before have so many experienced this painful type of loneliness. No one is exempt from it. I think of the loneliness of a child or the loneliness of a young person who goes off to college, or a young man or young woman in the first week of a new job. I think how easy it is for teenagers to get with the wrong crowd if it promises an end to loneliness.

You would think that marriage would put an end to loneliness. Many a partner is cut off from his or her mate because of pressures to succeed. I have married many young couples and I have watched brides' Christian ideals gradually wane because they're too lonely to maintain them. The husband simply has no use for Christianity. His friends despise religion and mock the church, so she refuses to worship and no longer prays.

Loneliness is no respector of age or situation. Youth are lonely. They experience a period of uncertainty and change in search of selfhood and independence. They often feel lonely and misunderstood. The loneliness of middle age is no less acute when one comes to grips with the harsh realities of frustrated dreams and lost ideals. And then there are the elderly who feel pushed off to the side of the mainstream of life. They miss their work, their children, and many of the things they once enjoyed doing. They spend most of their time sitting around someplace, waiting to die.

There are many ways people can be lonely. One of the most frequent is due to the physical absence of loved ones. Death is a common creator of loneliness. But there are other forms just as real and often as painful. One is the loneliness that comes with leadership. I'm sure the Oval Office is a lonely place. So is the minister's study. Any leader who makes critical decisions knows the kind of loneliness which comes with the territory of assuming responsibility. Jeremiah the prophet knew what it was to stand alone and make decisions that would affect other people when he said: "I sat alone, because thy hand was upon me" (15:17). Then there is the utter loneliness that comes with depression and failure: the loneliness of temptation, guilt, and doubt. This is why we live in a mixed-up world—we can be lonely in the middle of a crowd! Didn't Jesus feel the tug of a lady stealing up from behind in a crowd? She knew the loneliness of physical illness. But perhaps the worst form of loneliness comes from our sins, which brings loneliness to the soul. Sin separates . . . from our closest friends, from our families, from peace of mind, but worst of all, it separates us from God. Judas Iscariot knew this loneliness for John told us that after the supper Judas went out "and it was night" (John 13:30). It was night all right—in more ways than the sun going down. Judas had a blackout in his soul which can be more devastating than the darkest hour before sunrise. So loneliness is a universal experience and all of us experience its pain in varying degrees. No two of us travel the same road. Our experiences are uniquely our own, but every last one of us, with no exceptions, will know what it's like to be lonely, if we haven't found out already.

Loneliness is no stranger to biblical characters. In both Testaments we have examples of those who struggled with it. The psalmist presented words inscribed by a lonely soul (Pss. 23; 38; 88). Jesus knew what it was to be lonely. He knew it right in his own home. He experienced the solitariness of the wilderness of temptation. He sweat drops of blood in Gethsemane, and experienced the awful abandonment on the cross, when it felt for a moment that even God had turned his back.

Jesus' constant dealings with loneliness were mirrored in the life of his mother Mary, who perhaps experienced the greatest form of loneliness—struggling with that which makes no sense, namely, injustice. The amount of biographical material in the New Testament about Mary is meager. All we know is that she came from Nazareth and was obviously a part of the devout Jewish group who were steeped in the traditions of Israel. She lived with the hope that the Messiah would soon come and deliver his people. Where we really find out what Mary was made of comes from the experience that took place nine months before Jesus was born . . . the mysterious encounter between Mary and a messenger of God called Gabriel (Luke 1:26-56). Some kind of confrontation occurred and two incredible propositions were made by God to Mary.

First, she was told that she was "favored of God," but had no concept at that time all that being "favored of God" entailed. Surely Mary was surprised by this, but she must have been absolutely stunned at the second word, that she was to be the mother of the long-awaited Messiah! Having heard these promises from God, I'm sure Mary began to wonder how it was going to happen. At the moment of these revelations, Mary was engaged to Joseph, which from her perspective caused special problems. Nevertheless, Gabriel told her there would be no human partner in this act of conception. Just as in the beginning the Spirit hovered over the face of the deep and called forth life out of nothing, so now the very same Spirit would overshadow her and call forth from her womb life where there was no life, an act that was distinct and unique from all else to that time in history. Lonely? You bet Mary was lonely!

She was also a teenager, pregnant, and unwed. She knew how the tongues would wag. Maybe she had second thoughts and would just as soon not be "favored of God." Like sharks catching the scent of blood, moving in for the kill, busybodies would detect the scandal and viciously attack her reputation. But what would the rest of the people in Nazareth think? Mary knew what a straightlaced village Nazareth was; that there were no secrets, and everybody knew everything about everybody else, especially the spicy stuff. But what really bothered her was Joseph's reaction. What would he say? How on an earthly scale would she explain her pregnancy to such an upright man of integrity? Could she stand the scorn of the man she loved and planned soon to marry? Could so many nagging questions come from being "favored of God"? Would he believe her or the gossipers? Would he conclude she was a cheap tramp who had stepped out on him and got caught? Would he call off the marriage? Then what would she do? Where would she go? If Joseph turned her down, she knew she would be branded as an adulteress, and that could mean being stoned to death. And what would become of her baby? Ah, yes, the baby! "Throne of David . . . He will be called Holy, The Son of God"? What of Mary's baby?

Well, Mary really was pregnant. A plain peasant girl of Nazareth, engaged to a fine carpenter of the village, was to be the mother of the promised Deliverer! More questions . . . why me? Why did God choose me? Why not a rich girl or a proud queen? The questions brought more loneliness over her as she tried unsuccessfully to sift through the meaning of the announcement. She longed to talk about it with someone. But who would understand? Who would believe her story? Oh, if she could only get away from Nazareth! Then Mary remembered her cousin, Elizabeth. Elizabeth was a lot older than Mary and had become her second mother. Married to a priest for many years, Elizabeth had endured the loneliness and disgrace of being childless. Then, suddenly, at a time when she was beyond her childbearing years, Elizabeth discovered that she too was to be a mother. Mary knew that at least Elizabeth would be an understanding friend. Although she lived some fifty miles away, Mary set out immediately and burst in on Elizabeth.

Mary couldn't have selected a more understanding person than Elizabeth. She really used her head by going there and spilling her story. Sure enough, she received strength and encouragement from Elizabeth's mature faith and wisdom and Mary was helped through the early, critical months of her pregnancy.

Bolstered by Elizabeth's support and friendship, the lonely teenager returned to Nazareth, knowing that soon the entire village would know she would have a baby. She braced herself for the barbs and jokes and sarcasm as people counted up months on her. It would have been easier just to stay with Elizabeth in Judea, but as wise counselors are prone to do, she urged Mary to learn to stand alone. Thus, she decided to go back and face Joseph as well as the village people.

Sure enough, she quickly discovered that her worst fears were wellfounded. Joseph had figured she was carrying a child. She tried to explain, but her story held no water for the pragmatic carpenter. She hoped and prayed that Joseph would have some small degree of understanding, but no. The lonely teenager turned and ran away, disappointed that he could not understand. Luckily, Joseph was not a little man—of vengeance. He didn't intend to make a public spectacle of Mary's situation. He responded with compassion if not understanding, which is saying a lot, for he must have been hurt too. He did not want to "teach the young girl a lesson," but merely hoped she could somehow pick up the pieces of the broken shreds of her life and that he would be able to do the same. So Joseph went his way and Mary had no one left but God, who got her into this by "favoring her!"

Mary steadfastly trusted in God—there was no one left. Then Joseph appeared at her door. What was he doing there? He had come to tell Mary he had changed his mind, which was hard to do for a man who worked with tools instead of words. Joseph tried to express the inexpressible, that God had plans for him and Mary as husband and wife—and for Mary's baby! So this pregnant teenager, who had already been subjected to deeper fears and greater loneliness than any woman ever, accepted Joseph and agreed to commit her life and the life of her baby to the carpenter from Nazareth. Joseph told her they would name her baby Jesus, for he will save his people from their sins. Together they went forth to confront a life of transition and loneliness.

Now what can we learn from Mary's experience with loneliness that comes into our lives when we struggle with transition? I can see two things. When we are lonely, we can:

1. *Reach out to others.* This is the first sensible thing Mary did. During a time of intense emptiness I am tempted to retreat inward, but Mary's example of pushing herself to take the initiative and seek out a caring person like cousin Elizabeth was exactly the solution to her problem. And the same type of action can be a solution for you and me. No one is suggesting that this is easy. But we have to assume responsibility for our healing. Like when Jesus asked the thirty-eight-year-old cripple by the pool of Bethsaida, "Do you want to be healed?" He asked that piercing question because he knew that some people actually do not want to be independent. Some know it is much easier to remain in a dependent state and let others do it for them. I find it difficult when I'm feeling cut off, to ask a friend for some attention, but I think that to admit such a need takes courage. And that alone would put you on the road to healing. It also makes sense. You don't need to live in a family long to see that those who love us deeply often can't detect our innermost hungers. I think it's unfair to assume that someone else would. How could Elizabeth know what was happening to Mary? So Mary did the natural thing, she took the initiative by asking directly for what she needed and it was a most creative way to counter the loneliness she felt. Most of us, like Mary, sense that at times we are loners, although we have many

acquaintances but few real friends. We all need Elizabeths—persons who will give time and understanding. And I know of no better place, other than professional counselors, than church. Because in church, you and I don't have to stand alone. The resources of God are available, not as a shoulder to cry on or a crutch to keep us dependent, but a source of strength and understanding. This is not unlike that which was provided for Mary by Elizabeth, enabling her to break away from the bondage of loneliness. Thereby we can become our best selves which is hindered often because of our self-imposed loneliness.

Jesus felt the need of companionship. He chose the twelve so that they might be with him. That's why he was so sad when he found Peter, James, and John sleeping in the garden. "Could you not watch with me one hour?" That is the cry of a soul that is strong enough to stand alone, but is disappointed that he should have to be lonely.

Now we cannot intrude upon the intimacies of another's experience, but we can help, like Elizabeth did, once we are aware of a need. One of the first works of the Holy Spirit was to form the disciples into a church. They were not to be isolated individuals, struggling to maintain their faith on their own; they were welded into a committed community of faith. Because of that, one of the main tasks of the church is to be a home for the lonely—that is all of us. To our fear of being alone Jesus pledges the reinforcing fellowship of his church and says, "I will never leave thee, nor forsake thee" (Heb. 13:5, KJV). And "Lo, I am with you always, to the close of the age" (Matt. 28:20). So where else but church can we more naturally take the initiative to get what we need and ask directly for it? For as Mary's example reveals—it was one way to deal creatively with loneliness.

2. The next thing she did was to *actively receive the care* given to her by Elizabeth. Now this is important. On the surface it might appear to be automatic, but it's not. Someone offers another help and they don't accept it. That's right. I find that during times of strained or severed relationships, I am prone to

resort to self-pity and many others are the same. When that happens, anyone can try to help but it will be resisted and sometimes even rejected. People at a "pity-party" will actively resist positive attention. Didn't the rich young ruler do this very thing? He came to Jesus with a problem, asked for help, and when he got his answer turned away sad, consciously refusing help! At such times, and especially in transition, we tend to become self-centered and won't let others in. We make it difficult for others to give help. But not Mary. She not only went to Elizabeth, she took what she was given and was strengthened by it. And she didn't feel any compulsion to "pay her back!" Mary did the hard thing; she received with graciousness the help that was offered to her. When you feel alone, it's easier to nurse miserable feelings than to replace them with the positive affirmations available to us.

So Mary shows us how to stand alone and stand tall by actively receiving from those around us. That is why I admire Mary so much. She made the best of what she was given. It reminds me of my senior year in high school when our baseball team had advanced in the playoffs. I was on base, running for home plate after the batter got a hit. The throw made for a close call about the time I collided with the catcher in a cloud of dust, the umpire had to make the call. This famous southern umpire, Bob Deal, was also my neighbor and was sometimes affectionately called "Dirty Deal." Dirty Deal had to make the call. He had plenty of help. My coach was yelling, "He was safe!" The opposing coach yelled, "He was out!" And Dirty Deal yelled, "He ain't anything until I call it!" *(He called me safe.)*

This episode on the baseball diamond is a parable of life, and something we need to remember . . . life isn't anything until we call it, until we decide what it will be. It would be wonderful if we didn't have any close calls in life, if we could always have things like we wanted. But that is unrealistic . . . we have to make close calls. Living in transition means you will have to take life as it comes and make the best of it. Mary did it with her commitment to God, "Let it be to me according to your word" (Luke 1:38). With that attitude of commitment and courage to seek out a helper when she got in a pinch, and her graciousness to accept the help that was offered, Mary learned to stand alone.

It's the same with us. Nothing we have ever done or have ever had done to us can prevent our redeeming the past into some positive future. There is always a door that can be opened when every other door seems shut. The problem with so many today who have to learn to stand alone is the pessimistic belief that their shattered world must forever stay shattered. But it isn't true. It will only be shattered as long as they call it shattered! The sunshine always comes out after the storm. Just so, the business of living in transition is to somehow manage to survive the storms until the clouds pass over. Then you pick up the pieces and try to find a way to put them back together. That's difficult to do, but let's face it—we don't have many options available. You can wallow in self-pity like the thirty-eight-year-old cripple, go away sad like the rich young ruler, or knock yourself out in hostile resentment like Judas Iscariot. By so doing, you will be calling your life *miserable* and making it that way for everybody else around you. I suppose it's similar to what the famous basketball coach once said: "Things turn out best for those who make the best of the way things turn out." That's what Mary did. Now let us go and do likewise!

---

[1]Wayne E. Oates, *The Revelation of God in Human Suffering* (Philadelphia: The Westminster Press, 1959), p. 75.

11
Jesus: Minister While You Wait

I read once of a bored youngster who decided to build a hospital for butterflies. He made a wooden box and equipped it with a wire screen to serve as the hospital. But he had no sick butterflies. Consequently, he began to knock some of them down out of the air. The butterflies no doubt, needed his "butterfly hospital" to recuperate. Is this not a parable of the way we live? Most of us create our own meantimes and if so, we'd better learn how to maintain them.

There are all kinds of meantimes that we seek to avoid. People wait for inspiration to accomplish something spectacular. But in the meantime, life goes along and what they anticipated doing without drudgery is left undone. We wait for ultimate truth to hit us like a sledgehammer, but in the meantime we are forced to live as if something is true. Life turns its own corners and waits for no one. So we bet our lives on something. Nobody escapes these meantime situations. Thus, we wait to go someplace, read a book, research an idea, or become a new person. We end up letting our lives full of meantimes wash down the drain.

This is especially true religiously. It's much easier to passively believe that Jesus will someday rule the world, fill our stomachs, solve our difficulties, and wipe away all tears, than to be effective in these areas ourselves. The normal approach is to keep church-related activities nice and fuzzy and in the future. That way we won't have to deal with them. Our habit is to deny with our meantimes what we affirm in our eternities. But nothing is more with us than these meantimes of life. And nothing is overlooked as much. When we finish making our grand plans for the future, we stop and make this concession almost as an afterthought: "But in the meantime . . ."

Jesus knew that the meantime is where life is lived, where decisions are made, where pain is suffered, where we are lonely and tired. That's why he spoke to his followers about the "little while" that they had to live in—a time of his absence, a time of transition to another time, when they would see him and be glad. We know now that Jesus was talking about the time following his death and before his resurrection. I see it, however, as a universal symbol of all times of transition—that lonely stretch of desolation when the good seems to be absent and our dreams along with it. "Something is going to happen," he told them. "And I won't be around for awhile. But later on, you will see me again." Now we don't live literally in that same time of which he spoke, but I'm suggesting that we all experience the "little while," that time "in between," the interim meantime . . . which we live in most of the time.

Reminding us that most of life is lived in the "little while," one minister said: "All ages are restless ages to the people who live in them. All times are critical to the people who have problems. All roads are weary roads when we have too far to walk. People do not like to wait. This is a badge of our immaturity."

But like the disciples, we've all had to live, waiting for something: to grow to maturity, for surgical wounds to heal, for graduation, for the building permits to run their course, payday, a lucky break, quitting time, monthly installments to be completed, stocks to go up, for the letter carrier, or sometimes for the undertaker. As you can see, most of life is lived—waiting—in the meantime. And if we don't learn to live in it—we'll only be half alive.

And our church waits to leave the present building and enter a new one. What will we make of the interim period? There are more waiting rooms, long lines, and unanswered telephone calls than we like to think about in life. So life, if it is to be lived as we know it, must be lived while we wait—in the meantime.

The interim challenge has always confronted God's people, both individually and collectively. Israel waited forty years between Egypt and Canaan. The Jewish exiles waited seventy years in Babylonian captivity—yearning for the distant hills of Zion and their sacred Temple. It was the bloody four-hundred-year interbiblical period, between Malachi and John the Baptist which had the Jews looking under every stone for the Messiah. Was it Judas Maccabees? Simon the Zealot? Was it John? It was Jesus of Nazareth. But when he came, they didn't recognize him. That's what a mishandling of the interim can do to you.

Then Jesus himself faced the challenge of the interim—scholars call it "the silent years," referring to the first thirty years of his life. It was a time of preparation in Nazareth which he spent wisely. And what was the apostle Paul to do in the enforced interim of imprisonment in Caesarea and Rome? He wrote letters to his friends and churches he had established—which later became the bulk of the New Testament.

But by the end of the first century, the challenge of the meantime became particularly acute for the early church. They had been told the second coming of Jesus Christ would occur during their lifetime. But as time went on, nothing happened. Were they wrong? Or did they misunderstand the nature of Jesus' second coming? Nevertheless, it became apparent to the followers of Jesus in that day that they too had to reckon with an undetermined interim. What were they to do while they waited? Read 2 Thessalonians 3 and you'll find that some of them quit work, sold their belongings, and sat down to wait on Jesus. But Paul, who dealt with misunderstanding often, rebuked these as being lazy and said, "If any one will not work, let him not eat" (3:10).

It was during this difficult interim period of the church that Matthew's Gospel was written. My hunch is, that Jesus told three particular stories which gave them great hope and insight as he described what a Christian was to do while he waits—in the meantime. I'm speaking of the three parables in Matthew 25, about the wise and foolish maidens, the parable of the talents, and the judgment.

In each of these stories Jesus taught that what is done or not done while we wait, determines whether that for which we are waiting will be a blessing or a curse. How true that is! I know many teenagers who severely limit their futures because of misusing the interim between adolescence and adulthood. They couldn't wait to grow up and the meantime whipped them. How many folks do you know who are lonely and isolated because they're waiting for the "perfect friends" who are like themselves in every way—or the flawless community, or the perfect church? How many mid-life folks are drained and empty at forty, because they reached for all the gusto at once— rather than take advantage of the opportunity to learn and mature? How many Christians have failed to be salt and light because they're waiting for God to zap them off some mule like he did Saul of Tarsus? How many old folks have died shortly after retirement because they pushed themselves so hard in the working years that their health was broken and didn't have the ability to slow down without feeling guilty or worthless?

Jesus was right, what we do while we wait can make all the difference in the world between success and failure, joy and disappointment, light and darkness, life and death, heaven and hell.

And it is to this challenge of what to do while we wait that Jesus speaks in Matthew 25. Let's look at his instruction about what to do while we wait in the meantime.

1. *The Wise and Foolish Maidens (Matt. 25:1-13).*—This parable tells us we had better be prepared for a long wait. Perhaps this story is what inspired "Murphy," to write his law, which is: "Nothing is as easy as it looks. Everything takes longer than you think. And if anything can go wrong, it will." This is the lesson of Jesus' parable of the wedding feast. The wise bridesmaids were prepared for a long wait, but the foolish attendants didn't bring enough oil in case of a delay. And when the bride-

groom finally came, they were trying to buy more oil for their empty lamps. Consequently, they missed out on the party because they didn't anticipate that they would have to wait.

Maybe these were some of those who believed they'd be ushered into the kingdom of God immediately and didn't think they would have to live out their lifetime in the Roman Empire. But if they had been familiar with the Old Testament they would have known—the biblical story is about people "waiting on God" as he patiently works in love, with our freedom and willfulness. So in captivity the false prophets urged the Jews to rebel and fight against their oppressors, but Jeremiah said, "Don't believe them. It's going to take seventy years before the interim is over . . . meanwhile, plant gardens, get married, put down roots, and pray for the welfare of the Babylonians." Then—when you can do that, God will bring you back home again! That's how God works with his people. He gives them time to think about what they have done. And it took him centuries of preparation before he brought the Messiah to the world and he ended up, after three years of ministry, on a cross. Anybody who gets involved with the biblical God had better be prepared to wait! Don't expect the interim to end overnight —that is not the way of life as I know it. Be prepared for a long interlude—that's the way it is most of the time. Rarely do things that really matter, happen instantly. That's why such things as education, marriage, family, and salvation are processes that last an entire lifetime. There are no shortcuts to the kingdom. But this must not cause us to quit. We can't let this make us give up before the final curtain falls. With God there is always a future no matter how distant. We must be prepared to wait and psyche ourselves up to see what God will do in the meantime.

2. *The Parable of the Talents (Matt. 25:14-30).*—Jesus teaches us to use what we have, while we wait, in this parable. Three men were given different amounts of money by their master (1-2-5) before he went away on a long journey. After he came back, two of the men (2 and 5) used the talents they were given

and doubled their money to four and ten. The one-talent man was too security-minded and buried his talent for safekeeping rather than putting it to use and risk losing it. He lived by the slogan: "A bird in the hand is worth more than two birds in a bush." But that depends on what the bird is doing in your hand and what the two birds are doing in the bush! Nevertheless, he hoarded his one talent so that there was no increase for his master. Consequently the two- and five-talent men were praised and the one-talent man was condemned because he did not use the gift he was given.

The parable may be interpreted as a story about dead and lively money. Dead money is money which cannot be used. More exactly, it is money that is never invested in improving human life. Some people's money is dead. Other's money comes alive through risking wise investments. For those who take this risk, there is a reward. For those who hesitate, there is nothing. God gives people differing gifts. Thus, it's not what a person *has* that matters in life—but what he *does* with what he *has* that counts. Although we aren't equal in talent, we can be equal in effort. The one talent man was rebuked, not because he didn't succeed, but because he did not try. He simply did nothing with his gift. And what we don't use, we lose. If we are faithful, we will receive a reward—more responsibility! The reward of a faithful worker is not rest, but more work!

Jesus' second parable raised a question of what you are doing with what you have while you wait? What is it that God has given us to do right now, while we wait to enter a new building? The amount of time or the amount of talent is not the question. Nor is the fear of taking a risk or the fear of failure an issue. If you wait until you have more or for the right moment, Jesus says, "If you hesitate to become involved with what you have right now—you will miss the kingdom."

The greatest compliment Jesus ever paid anybody was to that lady who annointed him with her costly perfume and wiped his feet with her hair. He simply said, "She has done what she could." What are you doing while we wait?

3. *The Parable of the Judgment (Matt. 25:31-46).*—In Palestine the sheep and goats graze together in the daytime. At night the sheep are separated from the goats because the goats are affected by cold temperature. The sheep, however, prefer the open air at night.

Perhaps Jesus employed their practice of separation to draw an analogy of a screening test to which all of us will be subjected. We are accountable. We are going to have to answer for what we do. In this parable Jesus tells us we can occupy our meantime by ministering to people in need. This was one of the most vivid parables Jesus ever spoke and the meaning is crystal clear: God's yardstick for judgment is how we react to human need! We will not be judged by how smart we are, or the fame we've acquired, or the money we have—only by the help we've given to those in need.

Consider the kind of help Jesus expects from us. Spontaneous help, not acts, calculated to be good. The sheep didn't realize they were ministering to Christ when they met the needs of the lowly. Last week I let our dog Daisy out and she spotted a rabbit in our yard. Immediately she took off in an attempt to catch it but was unsuccessful. Nevertheless, you put a rabbit in front of a dog and you will find out what a dog is. Put a person in need in front of a Christian and you'll find out what a Christian is. Help in simple things is what God is interested in . . . things that anybody can do, like giving the hungry something to eat, or a thirsty man a drink, or welcoming a stranger, cheering the sick, visiting the prisoners. If you want to whip the meantime, try caring for somebody who really needs it! Jesus says there's salvation in it!

Psychologist William Marston tested several thousand people asking them: "What have you to live for?" He was stunned to find that 94 percent were merely enduring the present while they were waiting on the future. They were all waiting for something to happen; waiting for children to grow up and leave home; waiting for next year when the bills will be paid off; waiting for another vacation; waiting for tomorrow without realizing that all anyone ever has is today because yesterday is gone and tomorrow never comes.

I think Marston has captured an accurate truth. Life never stops. It is always moving and we constantly find ourselves waiting in transition from one place to another. Some of us are at different places, but we're all moving. You can never settle down. If someone says that to depart is to die a little, then to stay is to die a little, too. It is to remain attached to the same base instead of risking the leap to the next . . . as life calls us to go forward. We must always be letting go of where we are and moving on to where we've never been; leaving one place in order to find another, abandoning one support in order to reach another; turning our backs on the past in order to move on into the future.

So I don't know what waiting in the meantime does for you. But there's always an interim . . . it may be leaping from health to sickness. Or graduation. Or engagement. Or pregnancy. Or military service. Or the perfect job. Or between one success and the next. Or the line at the gasoline pump and the grocery store. Or between middle age and retirement. Or between divorce and remarriage. Between your loved one's death and your own. And our church waits, to leave this present building and enter a new one, meeting at the local Community Center in the meantime. What will we make of the interim? There are more waiting rooms, long lines, and unanswered phone calls than we like to think about in life. Whatever you're waiting for, if I've left anybody out, if it's not to be emptied of its meaning when it comes; you must meet the challenge of the meantime.

Jesus showed us how in chapter 25 of Matthew's Gospel. First, we can expect to wait and prepare for it. Next, we can do what we can with what we've been given. Lastly, we can minister to those in need while we wait. And that last parable about the sheep and goats tells us that while we wait for Jesus, he is in our meantime, encountering us. "As you did it to one of the least of these my brethren, you did it to me" (v. 40). While you wait—Jesus saves! What will you do while you wait?

12
Paul: Living
with Leftovers

Rarely do we face anything new in this life. Rather, it is our lot to arrive in the middle of things already in progress. We enter into our families, schools, and jobs that were here long before we were. Only the Creator knows what it's like to experience "the beginning." As we burst onto scene after scene in life that already has a history, we are both sustained and penalized by this fallout from previous years. Thus, we need to learn to live with leftovers. Living with leftovers involves a lot more than routine chores and day-old food. Our challenge is to learn to live in a leftover world full of inherited, leftover attitudes and problems of days gone by.

Because this is the case, one of the most agonizing problems caused by transition is that few, if any of us, live to see our deepest dreams come true. Not many individuals have the chance to live their lives on the basis of their heart's desire. Rather, we have to deal with the leftovers. I don't know of anybody who has not faced the agony of having his dreams shattered at some time or another.

For our instruction, I have chosen an epoch from the life of the early church which is transition at its best. The world's newest and most promising religion was expanding from a tiny sect within Judaism to the larger Gentile world. In that day when Christianity was young there was a lot of excitement and hope surging within the hearts of those destined to spread the good news of Jesus Christ. But many of those bright hopes were dulled, as is so often the case with crushed hopes in a leftover world. Here we find one of the most potent illustrations of the inescapable problem of living with disappointment during this period of religious transition.

> But now, since I no longer have any room for work in these regions, and since I have longed for many years to come to you, I hope to see you *in passing as I go to Spain,* and to be sped on my journey there by you, once I have enjoyed your company for a little. At present, however, I am going to Jerusalem with aid for the saints (Rom. 15:23-25).

There you have a simple account of a man familiar with hope. But if any man ever knew the meaning of aborted plans, Paul did. Five times he was whipped, three times with the rod. He was stoned once. Shipwrecked three times. He faced constant danger in his travels, from storms, his own Hebrew race, and others. He knew the hardship of toil and hunger, physical illness, and spiritual anxiety. Paul was a man well acquainted with adversity. Yet, here he is dreaming of one of the most significant events in Christian history—to take the gospel west to Spain. It was a dream that involved the transition of Christianity across continents from Asia to Europe. Paul planned to go to Rome, but only "in passing," for his main goal was to use Rome as a launching pad to send him forth to Spain. That was his first choice. What he got was leftovers in the form of a prison in Rome. He was fortunate to be there, for prison in Rome held a lot more promise than facing a mob in Jerusalem. What a glowing hope stirred within the heart of this great missionary! But he never saw his dreams fulfilled because of his daring faith in Jesus Christ and his determined efforts to bring unity between Jew and Gentile.

Paul, against the better judgment of his friends, persisted in taking a peace offering collected by Gentile Christians to Jewish Christians in Jerusalem during famine. He simply felt it was hypocritical to take a divided gospel to distant Spain. This desire to unify his religion was what got him into hot water. It just goes to show that nothing divides us as quickly as an effort to unite. So Paul did get to Rome, but as a prisoner, held captive in house arrest. But he never made it to Spain. Tradition has it that Paul was martyred for Christ in Rome. That was the end of the road for him and the last days of this great man's life provides us with a story of a man who learned to live with the leftovers of a shattered dream.

It wasn't that Paul didn't want to go to Spain. He couldn't go. Paul never was a halfhearted personality. He would have gladly gone to Spain if he were able. But his path was blocked; his plans for expanding the gospel were shattered by consequences beyond his control. But the point of this chapter is simply this: Paul produced his most significant service for God with these leftovers of a broken plan!

Wanting Spain and getting prison . . . how familiar that experience is to all of us! Life mirrors Paul's experience often. Wanting Spain and getting Rome is a symbol of everyone, for who has not set out for some beckoning Spain, some noble goal, only to learn finally, that he is forced to settle for second best? Always, as humans, our reach extends our grasp. To be able to accept prison in Rome, the broken plan, the leftovers of a disappointing expectation and turn it around and make of it the greatest opportunity we ever had—how few people know that experience?

I can identify with Paul here. During my teen years I acquired a noble goal to become an athletic coach. I chose this goal as a vocation simply because athletics was all I knew up to that time. A normal year for me was completely dictated by sports. My life revolved around the sports calendar. Spring was for high school baseball and spring football practice. In the summer it was baseball and softball league competition. In the fall, was football season and basketball during the winter. After much growth and progress as a budding young athlete, I was wiped out in my senior year by a major injury. It began to dawn upon me that I lacked the physical capacity to participate in college athletics. But I wouldn't accept it. I was determined to play and in the process reinjured the knee—this time permanently. I still wouldn't be deterred from the vision. I felt that in time my body would heal. About that time I was married and one of the earliest covenants I made with my wife was this strong desire to go to college and participate in athletics toward the goal of becoming a coach. She not only agreed but volunteered to work to send me through school. Then along came our first daughter, Bonnie. I decided to go to work and put my dream on hold for awhile. Upon accepting employment in a paper mill in South Carolina, I made it clear that this was only an interim arrangement until I could make enough money to get back on my feet and return to college. We even bought a mobile home so it could easily be moved back to school. Then we had our second daughter, Wendy, and I never made it to my coveted "Spain." Instead I was stuck in a paper mill in South Carolina. I know how Paul felt. So I got mad at God for giving me weak knees, thereby preventing me from doing the thing I wanted most to do. I finally got over that with help from my church community which straightened out my distorted theology. I decided to continue my goal as a coach, with one minor change. Instead of football, I would coach people in church. Rather than coach in a game, I would coach in life. I became a Baptist minister. That was in 1968; it wasn't my first choice, but it has become that.

I suppose anyone could share similar experiences. I don't know of anybody who hasn't wanted Spain, but ended up in Rome. As I quickly approach my forties I look back and see our youth coming along with their ambitions and plans for some glamorous Spain. I wonder what will they do when they face the inescapable experience of living with leftovers. What will they do when they are shut out of Spain and land in a jail in Rome because of external circumstances beyond their control? How will they handle it? Will they have the spirit and courage to take that leftover opportunity and make of it something better? We might do well to examine what Paul did that helped him turn a defeat into a victory. It may help us along the way.

First let's consider what Paul could have done. A lot of people don't digest their leftovers nearly so well as Paul. Instead, they get ulcers! This is because they let the frustration of being

hindered create a core of bitterness and resentment at the un-
fairness of it all. Such people grow callous and develop a strong
distaste for God, church, religion in general, and even for themselves. This is the path I was walking and there's no telling
where it would have taken me if it had not been for my church
experience. Living on a steady diet of leftovers can affect our
outlook on life. And because people can't get ahold of God,
they take it out on those nearby. They become cruel and mean-
ness describes their attitudes. They love no one and want no
love in return. They trust no one and don't expect anybody's
trust in return. They find fault in everybody and everything,
constantly complaining. Such negative people poison their own
souls and always harm themselves more than anyone else. A
biblical example is Judas Iscariot. Judas choked on leftovers and
his bitterness resulted in suicide.

Another common reaction to leftovers when hope is shattered is complete withdrawal into oneself. John the Baptist
withdrew into the wilderness and came forth preaching with
power. He did marvelous things to prepare for Jesus' ministry.
Unlike Judas, John was a high achiever and a servant of God to
be admired. But there are details of John's life that show he was
isolated because he separated himself from others. Mark describes John's ministry as: "The voice of one crying in the
wilderness."

When so many of us land in a Roman prison with our sights
set on Spain, we begin to pity ourselves, saying, "If only." "If
only I hadn't gone back to Jerusalem," Paul might have said. "If
only I had forgotten the peace offering and not given my all for
Christ. I could have been one of the most respected rabbi's in
the City of David right now. I could have had wealth, honor,
and life on easy street. But here I sit rotting away in jail. That's
what being faithful gets you!" But Paul didn't do that. Paul was
never bitter, indifferent, or detached. Many people today can't
cope with leftovers so they become too unconcerned to love,
too passionless to hate, too isolated to be selfish, too bland to
be unselfish, too indifferent to find any joy, and too cold to

experience grief. They are neither cold nor hot, just existing. This is the result of trying to escape from life and deny reality or fantasize it into nonreality. Paul didn't do that.

But what did Paul do? Several things probably contributed to his attitude. Not the least was his willingness to accept second-best circumstances and still cling to hope. This takes honesty to admit your dream has been shattered. You can't do this by withdrawing. I believe it is what Paul must have done, namely, honestly face the leftovers. He must have asked, "How can I use this liability and turn it into gain? What can I do, confined in a Roman prison, extremely hindered from reaching Spain?"

No doubt the event that Paul preached about caused him to consider this action. Paul spent his days and nights preaching about a God who can take anything that happens to us and weave it into his purpose if we will let him. It may cause us to be a little more understanding and lose a little pride, but Paul well knew the story of the cross where God took a tragedy brought about by evil people and made it the bedrock of redemption as Jesus exchanged his thorns for a crown. I would be the first to admit that this is not an easy thing to do, but I am saying it is possible. Whether you do it or not depends on what you're made of. But if you want to really live while you're alive and come to a constructive outlook while living in a leftover world, you're going to need this secret Paul discovered in finding victory over his situation. Paul never permitted these conditions to master him. "I have learned," he said, "in whatever state I am, to be content" (Phil. 4:11). Thus, he could stand tall in the face of the leftovers of life. There at Philippi, in jail, after having been beaten, chained, feeling tired and hungry, Paul sang the songs of Zion at midnight!

Ultimately then, I believe Paul's capacity to deal with life's leftovers was a result of his faith in God. Although Paul was physically alone, he knew he was not alone. For God dwells with us even in life's most confining limits. The Christian faith makes it possible for us to accept with dignity that which cannot be changed and to meet disappointment with inner confidence. Thus, it helps absorb the most intense pain without losing hope. This same Paul was the one who wrote that in life or death, in Spain or Rome, "We know that in everything God works for good with those who love him, who are called according to his purpose" (Rom. 8:28). No matter whatever else was shaken when Paul finally reached Rome, his faith was not. He still believed God had a purpose for his life there in prison. If God wanted Paul in Rome, then there must be something there worth doing.

Think about it. It's not until you hit bottom, get down and out, when the burdens lay heavy upon your shoulder and disappointment is ever so near, that you find out how real your faith is. Anybody can have faith when the sun is shining and the sky is blue, the birds are singing, the pocketbook is full as well as the pantry and the gas tank. Anybody can rejoice when the mind and body are free of aches and pain and the lucious shores of Spain loom out over the horizon. But if you find yourself flat on your back, down in the dumps, wanting Spain, getting Rome, and can still be sure there is some purpose even in that—then you know your faith is as real as Paul's was. I must point out that while Paul was the one who wrote the famous "in everything God works for good," I am not just impressed that he *wrote* it. I am impressed that he lived it. Indeed, he *made* all things work for good through his faith in Jesus Christ! So can we if our faith in Christ is real.

As I write this the walls of our new church building are being erected. I am thrilled each time I drive by because the place looks different. One day I noticed some extra pieces to hold the walls in place and allow the workers to get at the high spots. This is called scaffolding. The scaffolding on any new building is not attractive, but it is necessary while the construction is going on. When the building is completed, the scaffolding will be torn down and the beauty of the building will be prominent. In the same way, the circumstances of life are like scaffolding on a new building. It provides something to hold things up and stand on while we construct the building of our lives. One day we won't need the scaffolding anymore—the disappointments and the limitations. The second-best leftovers that come our way will be torn down. The God who can make all things new will teach us to regret nothing that has been a part of our history in his efforts to bring us to the likeness of his Son Jesus Christ. Like Paul said, "The sufferings of this present time are not worth comparing with the glory that is to be revealed to us" (Rom. 8:18).

If Paul's life showed us anything, it revealed that suffering, trouble, and disappointment aren't things that belong to other people. No one escapes leftovers, especially in transition. But how we handle these situations determines the quality of life as we know it. Disappointment itself is neutral. It shines on both the just and unjust. It can make or break a person, depending upon how that person faces it and handles it. It can bring you to defeat or inspire you to great victory. The latter route was the one Paul chose, because he was brave enough to look his leftovers in the face and dare to ask, "How can I transform this adversity into productivity?" Like the One before him who turned the cross into a throne, Paul asked, "How can I, confined in a narrow Roman cell, unable to reach the Spain of my dreams, change this prison into a pulpit?" And that is exactly what Paul did—change that prison into a pulpit with his pen; by writing the bulk of the New Testament which now inspires our lives! Paul's action reminds me of a little ditty I once read. Simple though it is, it might suggest an answer to how Paul was able to do that. It all depends on how you look at "disappointment."[1] If you take out the first letter and change the "d" to an "h" it then is no longer "disappointment," but "his appointment." Our disappointments can become his appointments. In reality, this is not something which a play on words can prove, it must be experienced to be believed.

Nevertheless, all of us are faced with leftovers in many forms. We slowly come to realize that we will never be the kind of person we had hoped to be, or our health hasn't held up the way we want. We reluctantly admit that our favorite dreams have not been realized; that some good friendships have faded; the years with our children have slipped away before we did all the things with them we had intended. These are the harsh realities of life that I've been calling leftovers, but we all have to face them. People respond differently to leftovers. Some avoid the issue, blurring reality with busyness. Others just grit their teeth and say unconvincingly that it doesn't matter. Some cover their pain with jokes. Some turn bitter and vent their hostility on those around them. But some, like Paul, find the grace to face the leftovers of life. They lose their illusions with an acceptance that is more than resignation; with a sadness that is neither bitterness nor self-pity; with humor that is not mockery; and with faith that life at its core is just like the Creator said in the beginning, "It is good!" When you can affirm the goodness of life even though it doesn't turn out the way you intended, then you have learned to live with the leftovers! I pray to God that this will be your response.

---

[1]John Bishop, *Courage to Live* (Valley Forge: Judson Press, 1976), p. 32.

13
Hebrews:
The Changeless Christ
in a Changing World

As I write the concluding chapter, the season speaks of transition. March and April are like bridges between the stark cold of winter and the welcome warmth of early springtime.

Where I live, nothing signals the arrival of spring any better than the famous Washington tidal basin cherry blossoms. Each year we get caught up in the suspense of whether the snow-like blooms will be at their peak by the scheduled festival. Past years have found the timing off a bit. They have either been too soon or too late.

I see in this spring fever hoopla a more eloquent message about renewal, hope, and permanence in a life of constant change. In Japan they juxtapose their cherry trees with stately pines, which speak of longevity. Then the evergreen is oblivious to seasonal changes. Furthermore, their gardens repeat the paradox of permanence in the midst of change by putting rocks in the middle of flowing water.

In Washington, we come close to the same imagery with the marble Jefferson Memorial that complements the transitory cherry blossoms. And we must not forget the Potomac River, grand paradox of permanence and change, which provides the same message. Transition brings with it this twofold word: permanence in the midst of change. Are not these things a necessary symbol for our rootless and migrant society?

Rollo May says so in his book, *The Courage to Create,* "We are living at a time when one age is dying and a new age is not yet born. We cannot doubt this as we look about us to see the radical changes in sexual mores, marriage styles, family structures, education, religion, technology, and almost every other aspect of modern life."[1] Nothing is permanent. Everything is temporary because . . . .

We Live in a Changing World

Things are not what they used to be. The good old days are gone. We live in a changing world.

Our customs are changing. A few years ago, death was an accepted, everyday occurrence. But the word *sex* was rarely uttered by any decent person. Then it was said in the alleys or accompanied by giggling because of our discomfort. But the taboo has changed from sex to death. We substitute the phrase "passed away" for death. Funeral cosmetics puts the mask of life on a cadaver. We surround it with beautiful flowers. We try to deny our limits and avoid our creatureliness until we've made an illusion of death. We've tried to rub out the boundary lines of death with rouge and lipstick. We live in a changing world. But there are some changes we can do without.

For instance, there is a certain kind of sexual liberation, which in one sense is necessary but we've gone too far with it. Pornography is widespread. We don't need that. When I was a kid, dirty magazines could only be bought under the counters at drugstores. Today they are sold openly. This philosophy has led to couples' living together without the commitment of marriage, as well as to the breakdown of the American home. You see it everywhere, at the theater, on television, in advertisements . . . everywhere. It is all nice and legal, for freedom of speech guarantees it in the courts, but you and I know this change is polluting the minds of our society and destroying our understanding of the decent side of life. We've lost the mystery of sex. It is no longer a mystery; it has changed to the purely biological function. We need to recover some of that mystery. We can know all about biological facts (which used to be called "the birds and bees"), but who can say what happens when a man and woman enter the boundaries of each other's personality? Sex in a human being is not the same as sex in a pig. Human sexuality involves both the biological and personal communication. Therein, lies the mystery. Today we're making it more and more an animalistic act and that's a change we can do without.

But this is a changing world. Politics are constantly swinging and moving like the flames in a fireplace. World powers change. The Arab states have 70 percent of the world's oil. They have the strongest capital position of any people in the world today. They can literally control the world's market. And that is new. For years the civilized world has laughed in derision at the backward Arab sheiks, with their big stomachs, sharp moustaches, and long noses. We picture them with women sitting on their laps, knees folded, inside their tents . . . a harem nearby, and a few gold Cadillacs for good measure. But we're not laughing anymore. Now the world's economy is virtually under Arab control. These desert dwellers, 6,000 miles away, can turn a nozzle and the wheels of industry in the West will grind down to a halt! And we find ourselves paying more and more to fill our gas tanks. All they have to do is stand on the hose and everything dries up. This is brand new! We live in a changing world. It leaves us confused and bewildered. Customs, politics, morality, world powers, May was right—they are all changing.

Our family purchased the house which had served as our congregational building for the last twelve years. Like Nehemiah we had some walls to rebuild, but made the switch fairly well with the help of some gifted men in our church. I guess you could say we live in a "converted house!" One of the things we have in our new home which we did not have in the former parsonage is a fireplace. I have certainly enjoyed our fireplace. I can sit in front of it and watch the flames for long periods of time and meditate. One winter day as I sat there warming myself, I noticed that it wasn't the fireplace that intrigued me, it was the fire. But both are necessary for fascination. Both the bricks and flames have form. However, the bricks are not as interesting to watch as the colorful, lively flames. The bricks are stationary. They never move. But the flames are constantly in motion, dancing around the wood. That is the reason, I guess, that I watch the flames instead of the bricks. Flames are a lot more attractive. But then it hit me, you can't have a fire in a fireplace without the bricks.

Human life, like the dancing flames in a fireplace has been marked by change ever since the beginning of time. Our day is no less so, thus the need for something steadfast like the bricks. That is what this book has been about, faith for an age of rootlessness.

Therefore, I would like to conclude by reminding us that in the midst of all these changes, there is that which does not change, namely, Jesus Christ, the pillar of the church. Like the steadfastness of bricks in a fireplace, according to the writer of Hebrews, "Jesus Christ is the same yesterday and today and for ever" (13:8). He is the compass that points in the direction that we ought to be mindful of. He is the "changeless Christ in a changing world." The one solitary life that has stood firm for nineteen centuries! How we need to experience that "Word" today! With all the changes, the slippage, and that which is in flux, we need the changeless Christ.

When I think of his changeless nature, I think of the conditions he came to change. The conditions haven't changed. From one generation to another, evil is still with us. We need to hear about the changeless Christ because every generation faces the same propensity toward sin.

Sin Has Not Changed

That's why those of every generation need a Savior just as much as the first generation. Every person born brings with him this tendency toward selfishness. The church calls it "original sin." But call it what you will, it's there. And somebody has got to be the instrument by which this egocentricity is turned into something else. The saving grace of the changeless Christ in a changing world is a necessity for wholeness in life for every generation simply because sin hasn't changed. Sin is still an offense against God. It plays fast and loose with the truth. It puts "other gods" before Jesus Christ. It is turning away from God toward self-sufficiency, pride, and self-centeredness. It leads to the diminishment of human personality. And all of this has not changed. It is ugly. It is evil. It destroys us. The Bible says, "The wages of sin is death" (Rom. 6:23). With two world wars fought within a generation and the clouds of a third looming dangerously low, we know firsthand what the Bible means by destruction. We've turned once too often to the "god of technology" and science has given us the very instruments that threaten to bring about universal annihilation!

This is a changing world all right, but sin has not changed because we have fabricated the Eleventh Commandment, "Thou shalt not get caught." It is cool to get by, but it's a sin according to today's standards, to get caught. It's all right to lie because we've taken Einstein's theory of relativity and applied it to the world of ethics. The relativity concept works fine in the realm of science, but it is devastating in the realm of morals. It does away with all absolutes. It's OK to steal if we can find a way to justify it. It is permissible to hate if we dress it up and make it look like patriotism. It's a changing world, but sin hasn't changed. People are still as mean and greedy and destructive as they were in Jesus' time. We use people and worship things and exploit each other and God's world. Paul was right, "All have sinned and fall short of the glory of God" (Rom. 3:23).

The Consequences of Sin Have Not Changed

When I was young, I used to be afraid of God and didn't think much about sin. But the New Testament has a serious concept of sin. It teaches us to fear sin and love God, but we sometimes turn it around and that results in alienation and destruction. Paul had a serious view of sin. Sin is to be feared, not God. It still tears down the spirit with guilt and depression. It destroys our personalities. It makes us ashamed to go to church and come before the presence of God. It makes it impossible to worship or pray. It tears us apart and fragments us into schizophrenics. It keeps us awake at night, disturbs our minds, separates us from all that is holy, and creates a living hell all around us. Sin still does that and it's consequences have not changed one iota. More people are emotionally disturbed today than at any other time in history. Many people have to have a therapist to exist. The psychopathic wards of our mental institutions are overcrowded. We read books on the bestseller list like, *Man Against Himself, The Neurotic Personality, Modern Man in Search of a Soul, Peace of Mind, How to Be Happy.* All this is the result of the consequences of sin.

Yes, we live in a changing world, but the consequences of sin have not changed. That's why the psalmist cried out after his sin: "Purge me with hyssop, and I shall be clean; wash me, and I shall be whiter than snow" (51:7). So you can change your hairstyle, the scent of your perfume, the length of your skirts, the size of your pants cuffs, and all the silly little things we do from one year to another. You can read dirty books, and travel to exotic places on fast airplanes, and buy big boats and do all the things people do to disguise the essence of life. But sin is still sin and the consequences of sin are still the same. "Do not be deceived; God is not mocked, for whatever a man sows, that he will also reap" (Gal. 6:7). That same Christ sin nailed to the cross 2,000 years ago is who we need today. It's a changing world, but he's the changeless Christ. Our sins don't change, nor does his grace change.

I once left National Airport in a storm. It was raining, the winds were blowing, and I was a little worried. We took off into the dark clouds and rose in elevation to 25,000 feet. All of a sudden we popped out into a whole different world. All the bad weather was down below and we just cruised along on top of the turbulence. There was the bright sun unmoved by it all. It seemed to say, "It's always better the nearer you get to me." And that same sun has been there ever since God said, "Let there be light." The same sun that dispelled the void of darkness on creation morning was the same sun that greeted me above that storm. The sun never changes. The clouds come and go. Rain falls. Thunder and lightning and the wind play like children at the sun's feet. Old "Sol" just hangs there rolling around heaven all day, keeping steady watch over God's creation. The sun has been around a long time, overseeing the procession of the centuries. It saw old Pharaoh enslaving the people of Israel. It saw Joshua marching around the walls of Jericho and Nehemiah rebuilding his walls. It seems that God has poured into one human life all the wisdom, love, and character that a person could contain as "the word became flesh" (John 1:14). There he stands as the centerpiece of all time, "Jesus Christ, the same yesterday, today, and forever!" (Heb. 13:8). Amidst all the changes and transitions of life, he is that which is changeless.

The nomadic tribes of Israel shunted from place to place, wandering around in the wilderness, often living in captivity in foreign places, with customs and religion that were different. But they held themselves together and maintained their identity only because they were confident that their God was unchanging, eternal, and never failing. I think you and I can learn something from their experience.

A frequent recurrence in the Old Testament is to the timelessness of God and his unchangeableness. The psalmist surely had this in mind when he said, "For a thousand years in thy sight are but as yesterday when it is past, or as a watch in the night" (90:4). The Bible holds to the conviction that with God, the past, present, and future are one. The first and last books of the Bible abound with this concept. Genesis has the phrase, "In the beginning, God." In the book of Revelation we hear the voice of God, saying, "I am Alpha and Omega, the beginning and the ending," (Rev. 1:8), "the first and the last" (v. 11). As this passage suggests, the New Testament Christians who founded the early church reflect this same conviction of the everlasting nature of God. And in a day when there is such rapid change everywhere and where individuals and families are frequently uprooted and migrate from one place to another, they are seldom in one place long enough to put down any roots, so the thinking goes. But we need to be reminded that there is something which is the same today as it was yesterday and will be like that tomorrow. Sometimes like the Christians at Corinth we are tempted to worship fabricated substitutes for God, which promises quick and easy dividends for our invest- ment of time, energy, and money placed at their altars. They entice us with the promise of pleasure, prosperity, and security and do it so effectively sometimes that we tend to forget the counsel of Jesus, "What shall it profit a man, if he shall gain the whole world, and lose his own soul?" (Mark 8:36, KJV).

But because this is a changing world, it is full of uncertainty. Which makes all of us easy prey to those who offer a gospel of easy answers. The "electronic church" abounds today because most of its prophets offer simplistic answers to complex prob- lems. They hook into our longing for a life without risks, iron- clad assurances, guaranteed retirement, and precautions for a future that may never arise. As a fellow "mobiphile," I can identify with that attitude. But despite the fact that we live in an uncertain world, there is one upon whom we can always depend. Paul put it this way, "for I know whom I have believed, and I am sure that he is able to guard . . ." (2 Tim. 1:12). I like that. It speaks with certainty. It is a sure word. There is no quibbling. Paul doesn't beat around the bush. He says he is absolutely sure of the One in whom he trusts. He is able to overcome evil. He is able to give the interior resources to con- front the trials and difficulties of a life lived in transition. Even that new taboo we mentioned earlier—death. He is able to overcome that too. God is able to offer us the only real security and certainty we can ever have in this life.

So every age has its period of transition. And the people to whom the book of Hebrews was written realized that they were living in a world in which old landmarks were disappearing. Those upon whom they had once relied for instruction were no longer around. Thus, the writer urged them, "Remember your leaders, those who spoke to you the word of God; consider the outcome of their life, and imitate their faith" (Heb. 13:7). Their security was gone, and there was only one thing left, "Jesus Christ . . . the same yesterday and today and for ever" (v. 8). Yesterday he gave his life to reconcile us to God. Today he is risen and exalted at the right hand of God. Forever he lives as "the Alpha and the Omega"; this same Jesus is all his people will need in any generation, facing every conceivable situation of this life or the next.

But these Hebrews had to learn a difficult lesson—it is a mistake to keep on trying to localize the universal God by putting him in a box, in the Temple in Jerusalem, or in the Holy Land. They never learned that while Christ is unchanging, he is at the same time, forever moving. He always leads his people to new ventures; always calls them to go out, like Abraham of old, not knowing where they are going, but only that it is he who is sending them. It is difficult to adjust to any sort of change. Because in any situation of change we stand to lose something and gain as well. This makes us reluctant to break with the familiar. We hesitate to let go of that trapeze handle.

Inside the camp of the old religion these Hebrews felt quite at home, totally insulated from the strange world of Jesus Christ on the outside. But they had to learn that this is where Jesus Christ is found, on the outside, claiming the strange, unfriendly world for himself. This faith in Jesus Christ is not something we can capture and tame. It is a dynamic process, always leading us to new challenges. And each new movement of God's free spirit tends to become stereotyped in the succeeding generations. We enshrine it in tradition, giving it the allegiance we ought to give only to God. But to be a part of the fellowship

of Christ today requires a forward-looking faith that the writer
of Hebrews called for. The recipients were living in a time when
the old and cherished faith was breaking up. Something newer
and better had come along and they just wanted to remain
attached. Consequently, they resisted attachment to the on-
ward-moving Christ.

We, too, live in such a world. Old familiar landmarks are
disappearing. Everything seems to be coming loose at the
seams. Our "leaders" are passing on. But Jesus Christ remains
the same and still calls for us to claim the new and unfamiliar
for his church today. It may be comfortable to build a tight little
compartment and construct walls to insulate us from the world;
content to see the same old faces, do the same old things, sing
the same old familiar hymns, and forget what is going on outside. But the old familiar patterns are constantly being exposed
to rapid change and dissolution which makes the world outside
in dire need of the unchanging Christ. Probably a more accurate
rendering of this chapter should have been "the changeless, yet
changing Christ." There is a changeless element about him,
which we deny with great peril. There are certain absolutes
about the nature of God that never change. It is in this sense
that Christ is changeless. But in another sense, there is a kind
of fluidity which prevents rigidness, concreteness, and the un-
alterable. There is the paradox of both continuity and disconti-
nuity. This is because our society is transitory. So the Word is
not only changeless, it is ever-changing because our words and
expressions are ever-changing in an effort to express the unchanging will of a God on the move.

Summary

We have been on quite a journey in our effort to document
man's search for a place during times of transition. We have
seen that mankind has always been concerned about his place
and God's. Ever since he was driven from his place in the
Garden, man has been relentless in pursuit of another. That's

what the history of civilization has been about, an attempt by man to make a place for himself, so he may regain his lost security.

He does the same with God. First he made an ark, a portable box, ready for immediate departure. It served as an early place around which he might gather to worship God. Then came the time when man wanted to build a temple for God. But God said no; he preferred a tent, for he was always on the move, that he was a God not bound by space. As God's people became settled in their Promised Land, a Temple was built and God had a special place—the "holy of holies." At last, man thought that he should worship in a permanent place, one that will never be destroyed. God's place will never be in transition again. But man was mistaken. The buildings built by human hands are never permanent. Life moves on.

Then came the day when man learned that God lives in a temple not made by hands. Jesus told the woman at the well that "neither on this mountain nor in Jerusalem will you worship the Father" (John 4:21). Rather, "God is spirit, and those who worship him must worship in spirit and truth" (v. 24). That is to say, God is universal. It is a lesson man needed to learn. But the lesson has been unlearned whenever folks believed that God was interested in that which is made with human hands. So the time came when people once again made buildings for God, such as the temples, and cathedrals with towering spires reaching to heaven. Sometimes they forgot that the factories, theaters, schools, and capitols belonged no less to God's world. They were content to keep God in the church. And those churches made of strong bricks have often become symbols of the permanence of God. But nothing is permanent except our forward-moving God who is now showing people that he will not be held within the buildings or social structures of the past.

If God dwells in a temple not made by human hands, maybe we need to see once again the God of the tent, for that might be a more profound symbol for our day than the God of the temple. Even today as our own church is being built to God's glory, we have used the concrete and wood and bricks and glass and plastic of modern society—not the animal skins used in framing ancient tents. But we must never forget that our building and all other human institutions are fragile and temporary. The God of history is on the move. Yet, in another sense, "Jesus Christ is the same yesterday and today and for ever." And people who serve him will be a people on the move.

I close with this last thought. As I reflect across the pages of GOD'S PEOPLE IN TRANSITION I can only conclude that the primary purpose for his people is not to get us someplace. It is to make something out of us along the way. Indeed this is Jesus' final word to the disciples in Matthew's Gospel (28:19-20). Most modern translations of the Great Commission are in the imperative: "Go therefore . . ." The phrase in the original is a temporal participle and can be paraphrased as follows: "While you are going . . ."

This is in keeping with the Old Testament. The Israelites learned as much *on the way* to Palestine as they learned anyplace else. Learning came in the process—"While they were going." And the character that developed through the struggle was what God was after. To reach any "Promised Land" we have to go through the wilderness, where the way is tough and lonely; where we are faced with the giants of failure, injustice, and crushed hopes. But while we are going let us never forget the importance of the struggle of the soul. It is not so much that we arrive at a place, but what we become on the way that matters. The experience of God's people in transition teaches us this: It's not what happens to us, but how we respond to what happens to us that really matters. Although the way may involve detours and be full of mistakes and conflict, hold to it and keep going forward. If you do, you won't be alone. For Jesus said, "and lo, I am with you always, to the close of the age" (Matt. 28:20).

Father, we thank you for the thin-spun web of our life, slung so precariously between light and darkness. On it, like dewdrops glistening in the morning sun, you hang bright jewels of awareness and yearning, of love and fulfillment—too great a burden of joy and wonder for such transience to bear. We praise you for Jesus who shared this transience in order to give us a new anchor in this life and the next. Upon his inexhaustible strength we dare to see the destiny of the whole universe turn; in him our fragile dreams become a solid rock. In his name, Amen.

---

[1]Rollo May, *The Courage to Create* (New York: W. W. Norton & Co, Inc., 1975), p. 11. Reprinted with the permission of the publisher.